Acclaim for Nathan Weathington's
Where the Hell Were Your Parents?

"A book for people who really, really want to believe *The Dukes of Hazzard* was a documentary."
— Jody Carrow, Editor In Chief, *The Claremont Review*

"*Huckleberry Finn* meets *Red Dawn*. Comic genius mixed with Southern Charm and downright hooliganism."
— Bennett R. Coles, winner of 2013 Cygnus Award for Military Science Fiction

"Nathan Weathington makes a good case for himself as a published writer and exceptional humorist, and I find most of his outspoken observations to be both substantive and relevant to the times. He has stand-up candor, great witty humor and at least a tongue-in-cheek sense of self-deprecation."
— Chanticleer Book Reviews

"My husband just read this book for the third time. I've never actually seen him read a book. I honestly thought he couldn't read."
— Michelle Becker

"The helicopter has crashed in Bremen, Georgia!"
— Carol Hogan

"Side splitting laughter. I haven't turned that many pages in a book since college, seriously."
— Joel Huggins

"Weathington pumps out cheap morphine chuckles in liberal doses."
— Chris Warner, author of *A Tailgater's Guide to SEC Football* and *Bushwhacked at the Flora-Bama*

"Truly one of the funniest books I have ever read in my life. It's about real boys acting the way boys would act when left to their own devices…and plenty of ammo. Just when you think it could not possibly get any more absurd, it does. A very smart enjoyable read."   — Kacy Pollak

"Ridiculous far-fetched, hillbilly nonsense. I've read it twice, and it just gets better and better. I truly spent the whole book wondering, where the hell were this kid's parents?!?"
— Kristen

"It is wildly fun, definitely destructive and somehow inspiring. This laugh out loud, crooked path of empowerment will inspire you to give your children wings, though certainly not angelic!"
— Kelly Denton

"If you ever wondered how frog-gigging, fireworks fetishes, and a willingness to test the law can produce upstanding, self-reliant guys (with a pretty sharp sense of humor), you'll crush this book in about an hour. If you like your junior memoirs more along the lines of *Little Women*, go and play around with some fireworks first before buying."
— D. Glasson

"It's hard not to identify with these little punks giving it to the man."
— Zackary Black

"A cross between a Norman Rockwell painting and an NRA poster - truly hilarious. Weathington nails it." — Nick

"If you think David Sedaris, Chuck Klosterman, and professional wrestling are funny, you will find this book is hilarious."
— Melissa

"Hilarious redneck shenanigans." — Marla

"The legend of the Weathington twins still hovers over our little town like the smoke from an enormous accidental forest fire."
— CBH

"A guilty pleasure of a read! Coming of age stories that skirt the law and good taste." — Jerome Black

Look out Foxworthy, this Weathington guy could be the new funniest man in the south. — D.A.B.

"Just the right amount of wrong. Quick-witted, expertly paced comedic memoir." — Geoff

"The funniest thing I've read in a long time. A great story teller. The pace is fast, and the stories are hilarious." — M. Moore

"I'm not sure I've ever read a book where I laughed more out loud than I did this one. It nails what life is like growing up in a small town in the South, and its portraits of the Weathington boys and their fellow hellions makes you feel like a kid again."
— J. Roe

"Truly legendary, Weathington's work raises the bar on how badass boyhood should be as a whole. Definitively sets the standard."
— Ben Falk, author of *The Resilient Farm and Homestead*

"Money well spent, however it did make me feel like I failed as a child."
— M.I.

"This book kills me. Does that make me a bad person?"
— Jaded Musician

"Delinquency at its finest!"
— V. Santos

"A rousing, rough-and-tough romp through The Deep South."
— Scott Aland

"Hilarious, disturbing and downright naughty!" — Ella Lawton

INVASION
OF THE
BASTARD CANNIBALS

AND OTHER TRUE STORIES OF A SOUTHERNER
BEYOND THE MASON-DIXON

by

NATHAN WEATHINGTON

PROMONTORY
PRESS

Invasion of the Bastard Cannibals
Copyright (c) 2016 by Nathan Weathington

All rights reserved. No part of this book may be reproduced or transmitted in any form by any means, electronic or mechanical, including photocopying and recording, or by any information storage and retrieval system, except as may be expressly permitted in writing from the publisher or the author.

Promontory Press
www.promontorypress.com

ISBN: 978-1-987857-69-6

Typeset by Edge of Water Designs, edgeofwater.com
Cover design by Evan Pine Design

Printed in Canada
987654321

To Morgan:

Thank you for allowing me to publish this book without having to run the jokes by you first. And thanks for backing me on every ridiculous endeavour I come up with.

INVASION
OF THE
BASTARD CANNIBALS

CONTENTS

Preface..xiii

Part I: We're Not in Georgia Anymore
1. Invasion of the Bastard Cannibals........................2
2. The Emperor's Banana Hammock........................13
3. Hippie Hygiene..20
4. Phallic Delight...32
5. Carnies Make Great Babysitters.........................41
6. The Stay-at-Home Dad Experiment.....................48
7. Never Go Full Hippie.......................................56
8. Riding Bareback, Bareback................................63

Part II: The Throwback Stories
9. The Raccoon Removal Scam: 1983, Age 9..............70
10. The Second Slingshot Incident: College................78
11. Poaching..83

Part III: Return to the Motherland
12. The Meat Rocket Incident of 1999......................92
13. Ebony and Ivory..104
14. Jesus Goes to Bed at 11:30.............................118
15. Sodomy, What Is It Good For?.........................131
16. The Inconvenient Truth About Men...................137
17. Mic Drop...145

Acknowlegements..153
About the Author...154

PREFACE

So here we are, volume two of my nonsense. I decided this book needed a little preface for a couple of reasons. First, it just seems like something a real writer might do while smoking a pipe and saying something smug about character development. And second, if you're a fan of my first book, you might be expecting more delusional Hazzard-esque type stories. There are a few of these throwback, hillbilly nonsense-type stories that many victims and witnesses insisted should have been in *Where the Hell Were Your Parents?* but a man only has so many *Shit Bomb* stories.

And, little known fact, I've barely had a speeding ticket as an adult. Yes, I peaked at ten. This is somehow both cool and depressing at the same time. I'm not sure how I went from being one of the most badass (at least in my mind) ten-year-olds on the planet to a man whose idea of a good time usually involves hot chocolate and fly-tying.

Luckily, if you move someone from rural Georgia to the

hippie-infested left coast of Canada, the jokes write themselves—no felonies necessary. You don't have to be Vonnegut to make a retired stripper from a vegan strip club who is riding a horse bareback with no clothes on funny. She makes herself funny.

So, here is your official warning. This book takes place when I'm an adult, so the subject matter is more carnal: hippies, doodoo, sex, scrotums, nipples, and coffee enemas among other things. Now, I've cleaned up my language quite a bit, but the subject matter you deal with as a twenty-four-year-old bartender in Florida is slightly different than as a ten-year-old in Bremen, Georgia.

You should also probably read my first book. That way I'll finally be able to splurge on those Truck Nuts I've been eyeballing for my Subaru, and also because you'll then have a more in-depth understanding of some of the characters in Part II of this book. But don't worry, this book stands alone and I'll be sure to reintroduce everyone as I go. Yes, I'm that good.

For the love of God, please turn down your political Tourettes before you read this book. There is nothing worse than someone who ruins a good joke by politically analyzing it until they have squeezed out all enjoyment from life.

And also please drop the offended act, especially you Southern debutantes. We have this thing now called the Internet: it transmits twenty-four hours a day, seven days a week, all matters of high quality smut and debauchery to a gadget in your pocket, so spare me the one-act play, Scarlett.

PART I

WE'RE NOT IN GEORGIA ANYMORE

1

THE INVASION OF THE BASTARD CANNIBALS

Being asked to ream out your wife's vagina with salad dressing is not normal. Not even in Canada. You read it here first.

I left The South in 1998 and have stuck out like a platypus ever since.

In a fortunate turn of events I ended up teaching high school math in the Bahamas for four years. Our school was extremely isolated; we would go months without seeing anyone from the outside world and therefore the faculty break-room quickly turned into a perverse Noah's Ark as the fear of celibacy set in.

In general, this was a good-looking bunch of people. Unfortunately, many of the women had already located their Ark-mate or found me slightly to extremely annoying. I was running out of options fast and decided to snag the next girl straight from the boat before she had a chance to really get to know me. My future wife hadn't unpacked her bags when I moved in for the kill. By the time she finally walked into the party, I had nervously drowned my small bit of game with a case of island beer. I flopped miserably, we had a huge fight, and, in hindsight, maybe I should have tried it sober and not while on a date with another woman.

Several months later, after the burn had faded, she came crawling back. Whether it was my charm, good looks, or the fact that I was the only single man taller than her within a hundred miles didn't matter. I soon found myself on the west coast of British Columbia as a married man—that's Canada, not the small British colony that provides the Brits with most of their blow. Vancouver Island is as far as you can go to the left, both geographically and in your tolerance of B.O. and patchouli.

Before moving to Canada, I had always considered myself a bit of an undercover hippie. I worked to save the world for a few years, owned some Birkenstocks back in the summer of 1996, and even tried fasting for a complete afternoon once. Now, I will admit that I've always been a regular bather, so it's not like I changed my name to Spirit Wolf and sat around a campfire discussing my past lives. (Here's a deep thought for you reincarnation folks: There are ten times more people on earth today than a few hundred years ago. Therefore, the spirit, chi, being, energy, or whatever you want to call it, that has found its way into your gullible body is only a tenth of the original. It's pretty watered down—the Miller Light of souls, if you will.) But when I landed in igloo country, it didn't take me long to figure out that I was a little closer to the Ronald Reagan end of the stick than I had previously thought.

All of my wife's siblings and their "partners" had gathered in Victoria for the Thanksgiving holidays (oddly, they do not refer to it as Canadian Thanksgiving). In western Canada, the term partner is used instead of the more easily defined husband or wife for good reason. Canadians get married half as much as Americans, and subsequently the vast majority of Canadian kids are bastards. Feel free to look up this little factoid before sending me hate mail, eh?

We Southerners get married fast and early because pre-marital sex is sinful, and a shotgun wedding is a good way to cover up an unplanned pregnancy. I've never quite followed the logic of these cloak and daggers. Are they trying to fool God or the grandparents? Having a baby out of wedlock is a country club *faux pas*, not Biblical scripture. You can't retroactively mend the broken Word of God; it doesn't quite work like that. The Bible is not a Mr. Potato Head. You don't have to be Encyclopedia Brown to figure out this charade. Southern girls have a subscription to *Bridal Magazine* when their potential husbands are still playing with blocks and eating their own boogers. Therefore, if a southern girl throws together a complete wedding in two weeks with a man who was last seen slurping tequila out of her navel at the Redneck Riviera, everyone knows she's got a biscuit in the oven. Plus, if you don't live in Mississippi, your kids will hopefully be able to count to nine one day, so they're going to uncover your sins no matter how much you disguise them. Plus, today's parents don't have the luxury of grainy, blurry, black and white photos to hide a pooch belly or the clenched teeth and flexed jawline of the father of the bride who is paying for a shotgun wedding between his pregnant honor roll daughter and Bobby, the nacho cook.

It appears gays and lesbians originally used the term "partner" when they were forbidden to marry. This law was written to protect wholesome family values by a somewhat heterosexual Christian senator who screwed prostitutes and beat his third wife. So the term went from describing people who could not marry to people who would not marry.

Morally, I don't give a damn, but I do find it odd and confusing. You can have a business partner, a tennis partner, a dance partner; and somehow, the woman who squeezed your melon-headed son out of her peepee is also a partner. It's too vague. Maybe we could start using the term unwed wife. It doesn't roll off the tongue, but neither does fiancé, which is snooty and sounds like you're ordering dessert at a fancy restaurant. I'm not sure what they're rebelling against. "It's just a sheet of paper, man." Yeah, exactly, so go pick it up and save us all the wordplay.

During a drunken night of poker, one of my close friends was feebly defending his stance on the subject. It started with the standard sheet-of-paper argument, but after the famous B.C. Bud kicked in, he started to open up.

"To be honest, I'm afraid of the commitment, man. I mean, one woman, forever."

Everyone else was high as well, and just nodded.

"Pete," I said, pointing out the obvious, "you share a mortgage and two kids with Susan, and you've had your nuts snipped.

You're just too stupid to get some free dishes out of the deal."

When he sobered up, he knew I had a point, and they were soon engaged. Although they are still engaged twelve years later, I feel I did my part to curb the bastard epidemic threatening the great country of Canada.

Southerners are very reserved people. Like icebergs, if you're at a dinner party in The South, you might only see ten per cent of a Southerner's true personality. The other more interesting 90 percent is buried under mint juleps in an ongoing effort to see who can blend in the best. Unfortunately, what's left tends to be the "How's your golf game?" type conversations that are so boring they make men named Phillip seem interesting. Southerners are great storytellers, but our stories are reserved for hunting camps and country juke joints, not the dinner table. We also do not discuss our sex lives at the dinner table, especially with the in-laws, especially with the wife's dad.

Back to Canadian Thanksgiving.

"Work is going well and we're digging the new house," I commented as the organic, shade grown, fair-trade emaciated turkey hit the table.

"I'm just ready to get this baby out of me," my very pregnant wife followed.

The conversation continued around the room and stopped at my sister-in-law's unwed husband.

"We're trying to get pregnant," he announced as if he were discussing his lawn.

Nobody flinched, not even his vessel's dad. Surely I had heard incorrectly. It sounded as if he just announced, at a formal setting, that he was screwing this man's unwed daughter in hopes of getting her pregnant. Her two older brothers didn't seem fazed as one asked for the delicious Yorkshire pudding (the more sophisticated version of a gravy and biscuit).

"That's great news, guys," the father said. "Congratulations."

Excuse me? What the hell? Trying to blend in, I sat silent. What do you follow this comment with? "So, what positions ya trying? The wheelbarrow? The rodeo clown? Two dogs chasing one tail?" (Not that you can get pregnant from that.)

I was baffled. When my wife and I were alone I let the questions fly.

"Is it just me, or did Jim just tell us they're trying to get pregnant?"

"Yeah. I'm excited for them."

"Okay, let me put this another way. Did Jim just tell everyone they're fuckin'?"

"You're so crude."

"Sorry. Having sex. That's weird, isn't it?"

"No. It's beautiful."

"You're messing with me, right?"

"What's the problem? We're pregnant."

"First, we are not pregnant. You are pregnant. Pregnant means you have a fetus in your womb. I looked it up after our last argument. I have no clue what a womb is, but I'm pretty sure I don't have one. Second, we're married. Third, there is a difference between saying we are pregnant versus trying to get pregnant."

"This isn't Georgia, Nathan."

"No shit," I said, wondering what I had gotten myself into.

At this point I began to seriously question my morals and ethics, as well as my personality as a whole. Maybe I was a "conservatron."

Over the next day I wracked my brain for another meaning to this dinnertime announcement. Maybe there was more involved in trying to get pregnant. Was it just sex? Was a doctor involved? Ribs? A box of wine? Canada is pretty white—maybe they were accidentally mistaking Barry Manilow for Barry White, a guaranteed sperm count killer.

Feeling confused and a bit like Bill O'Reilly in my new surroundings, I called my twin brother Brian back in Greenpond, Alabama, to check in and make sure I wasn't cracking up.

"No way," he said. "You must have misunderstood him."

"I double-checked."

"Wow. It's like a foreign country up there."

We contemplated how it would have played out differently back home; or, more precisely, who would have gotten to him first. We agreed it would have been more of a *GoodFellas* style beat down with Brian and me holding him while my dad whaled on him with a gravy boat.

The gravy boat domestic between my in-laws never came. I let it go. I had more important issues to deal with: prenatal classes.

"Why am I goin' to this again?" I asked.

"You're gonna help me deliver this baby," my wife explained.

"Don't you have to go to med school for that?"

"We also have a doula, so don't sweat it."

"Is that that Indian pig-in-the-blanket thing? I love those."

"That's a Samosa, dumbass. A doula is a birth assistant."

"Why am I goin' to this again?"

"Shut up and get in the car."

"Can we at least stop and get some samosas on the way?"

I was extremely embarrassed that my wife's dad knew she was pregnant (notice I did not say we). We had been married for four years, but to publicly display the fact we had indeed had sex left me uneasy.

When the prenatal instructor walked in wearing a muumuu, I knew I would not make it out alive.

Ten couples walked into the windowless room. I scanned the room for escape routes; the bathroom was inside the room, so the fake diarrhea play was out, and the exit door was directly behind the muumuu-clad Refrigerator Perry. I was trapped.

Day 1: I almost spontaneously combust from boredom as The Fridge told three hour-long anecdotal stories to cover each bullet point. She had two hours of material tops, and stretched it into four days so my wife would pay her $400.

Day 2: I lay down and took a nap. Why not? This lady was explaining that a baby came out of the vagina. Even I knew that—I'd watched *Wild Kingdom*.

Day 3: Small nap. Escaped straight past The Fridge for a trip to the bookstore and a much-deserved barbecue sandwich. Let a small brisket fart slip and pretended the homely pregnant lady with the cankles next to me did it.

Day 4: It gets freaky.

"There're many options for the placenta," The Fridge told

the class.

"What's the placenta?" I whispered to my wife, not wanting to know the answer. After hearing her response, I knew this was going to be the turning point in our marriage.

"How do we store it if we're going to eat it?" asked the pasty man who still looked like a virgin.

I sat frozen. Was I in a dream? Had I been drugged? I was blindsided. Canadians are cannibals! You'd think we would have covered this tidbit of sustenance in geography class or, at the very least, debated and discussed the oddity every four years during the winter Olympics. Did these people eat their tonsils, appendix, and foreskins? It was like science fiction.

As I fidgeted for my passport, my wife assured me we would not be eating the afterbirth. The cannibals continued to discuss recipes and how microwaves were the tools of the devil and obviously invented by Americans to slowly sterilize all Canadians in hopes of stealing their delicious maple syrup. (I do have to side with my Canadian compatriots on this one—I've never fully trusted microwaves. That being said, I find microwaves are kind of like prostitutes: if they happen to already be in the kitchen, you might as well slap a Hot Pocket in there.) As I started to dry heave, the conversation took a turn for the worse. Yes, it could still get worse than eating afterbirth.

"What can we do to prevent tearing?" said the other narrow-shouldered man, in a statement that should never be uttered by a man unless he's discussing the finer points of keeping a buck's hide pristine for mounting purposes. He struck me as someone who would easily follow a cult.

My head was throbbing as I continued holding my breath.

"Perineal massage is the best way."

"Shoot me straight, what's a perineal?" I whispered to my wife through clinched teeth.

"The taint," she responded, trying to reestablish our marital bond by engaging me in my own lowbrow vocabulary.

"Your husband should use extra virgin olive oil."

Skipping over the obvious irony of the chosen lube, it was time I stepped up and led my people.

"Let me get this straight," I declared in my best Captain Kirk authority voice. "Are we seriously talking about husbands reaming out their wives' vaginas with salad dressing?"

"Nathan!" my wife yelled as she slapped my leg.

"I would not have put it so crudely, but yes," said The Fridge.

"Really? Out of everyone here, I'm the only one? Nobody?"

The cult member guy explained that he and his wife find it arousing, which led me to believe he must have been screwing a rhinoceros before he met his wife. I might have understood if they had been using Crisco or lard, but olive oil? I can barely eat Italian food to this day without picturing that shiny-faced couple.

"You guys are messing with me, right?"

"I'm sorry you find this disturbing, Nathan. Try to open your mind."

"Maybe you should close yours a bit," I snapped.

There was a painful silence as my wife's nails dug deep into my leg. As I tried to remember if I had taken the red pill or the blue pill, the man who had not uttered a word for four days stood.

Now, *this* was a man. He was a Finnish commercial fisherman and carpenter who rolled his own cigarettes with his meat hook hands during our breaks. His body and face appeared to be chiseled from stone with a dull shovel, and his breath-taking hair was a shiny angelic blond. I would have ditched the fishing career and worked that hair if I was him: shampoo model, typecast Viking, or possibly just travel the country fulfilling horny housewives' Thor fetishes.

With my wife labor-breathing in the background and one hour left in the class, all eyes fell to the striking man standing in the middle of the circle.

"The way I see it," he said in his deep gravely voice as he strolled past The Fridge, "we should just be out back chopping wood."

His wife burst into tears, and I followed after my first Canadian friend.

By the time my wife found us at the pub drinking a beer, she was steaming. Deep down, though, she knew I was right. But she was still unwilling to admit that maybe, just maybe, cannibalism and post-hole digging were not part of a successful healthy marriage.

2

THE EMPEROR'S BANANA HAMMOCK

My dad, although retired for almost a decade, is still a football coach. I've yet to hear anyone refer to him as Mr. Weathington. He is Coach Weathington, or simply Coach. His ability to convince un-athletic white kids they could actually win football games is legendary. Along with his players, who thought him a god, he began lifting weights before people really had a name for it. With the seniors' discount at the gym, he is still able to bench 300 pounds and hike for three hours a day. The man is a beast.

No Atkins, no South Beach, no meditation, no excessive stretching, no raw food nonsense, and definitely no slow kung fu in the park.

I inherited my fitness sensibility from my parents—my dad in the weight room and my mom at the dinner table. Growing up in the Deep South, I was lucky to have the only health-conscious mom in the county. Don't get me wrong; she can slap together some fried chicken that'll make you question your sexuality, but only on special occasions.

Philosophically, I would say the idea of paying to go to a room, lift a chunk of steel, and then set it down seems strange, especially to my depression-era grandfather who single-handedly farmed 500 acres. Weight lifting may seem strange, but walking around in a sweaty, see-through, bright yellow banana hammock is something different entirely.

In British Columbia, people have a different idea of fitness. For the most part, everyone is white, which tells you right off the bat they will not be seen on the podium during the summer Olympics anytime soon. Canadians excel at hockey, bobsled, and all other sports that are too cold for people below the 49th parallel. All the medalists at the last winter Olympics looked like sailing regatta on their way to a Jimmy Buffett concert. Ski hills attract rich white people the way a mud bog attracts frayed denim. For the record, I am also white, and contrary to Hollywood and Larry the dumbass Cable Guy, not all southern males are racist, homophobic, sexist, or ignorant. Larry the dumbass is from Nebraska, by the way. He is not even Southern, or funny for that matter.

This paleness has given Canadians a heightened sense of sporting prowess. I'll spot you Steve Nash, but most Vancouver Island residents confuse being in good shape with being a good athlete—lots of triathlons, 5Ks, and bike racing, if you know what I mean. I'm no Bo Jackson, but I at least know the difference (although I would challenge David Sedaris to a calf off).

The term "world-class athlete" is thrown around loosely here. Just to set the record straight, if you are white and running any distance between 40 and 400 meters, you do not have world-class speed. At best, you have world-class white guy speed. The concept of world-class white guy speed was clearly defined in the *Adolf Hitler vs. Jesse Owens* case of 1936. White people are good at plenty of things; running fast is just not one of them. Affirmative action does require that there be one white dude in the 100-meter dash in each Olympics, and if he ever makes the frame of the photo finish, I will reconsider my stance on the subject. And I am NOT implying that black people are only good at being fast; I just mean that if zombies are attacking, odds are white people will be bait and black people will be running the planet.

Stretching is a big deal here in western Canada, so much so that it's apparently considered exercise in itself. In a moment of weakness, I was once convinced to join a father-son yoga class, which ended in what my wife calls "the yoga incident."

I have since sworn off yoga. The yoga instructors don't get that some guys, ironically the ones who need it the most, can't even get into the poses, much less work them for five breaths. These instructors are the same yoga enthusiasts who routinely post scantily clad pictures of themselves in yoga poses on Facebook. Nothing says *namaste* like sharing a photo of your half-naked body as you suggestively spread your legs for a few billion of your closest friends.

I also love it when they double down on the nana-nana-boo-boo pose by taking the photo at the beach. We are living in a bit of a perfect storm for people who hide all their insecurities in their hot bods—and yoga is cashing in. Our western ideals of competition, mass consumption, and over-sexualizing have pushed this ancient exercise to the pinnacle of its popularity. We also have these giant narcissistic machines that we can use to show our friends, our friend's friends, and our friend's friend's friends how cool we'd like our day-to-day lives to be. Put all this together and you pretty much have the perfect excuse to finally show everyone your perfect apple-shaped ass.

"They crank the heat in the room and all the moves are fast," my wife said. "You'll like it."

"Are you sure?"

"Trust me."

This was the last time I ever trusted my wife.

For the second and last yoga class of my life, it was easy to find my exercise clothes: t-shirt, stretchy loose mesh shorts, white crew cut socks, running shoes. I showed up early to make sure I got a place at the back of the class, just in case I had to pull the "I'm a volunteer fireman" exit.

The joint filled up fast. Everyone knew each other and the room was giddy just like before an orgy (or so I've heard). There is a huge spandex craze going on up here, like the '80s but much more expensive. This is the best thing that has happened to asses since the Thigh Master. All these gorgeous women were showing up to class in casual sport lingerie. At this point I started checking out my male competition. Clearly I should have shaved and plucked a little more. The men were uncomfortably better looking than me. They were hot in that

"I'm fun to take to an art gallery, but not to drywall your basement" kind of way.

Class began. Things heated up. Fast. First, the women started taking off a layer from their already barely-there outfits. The room was now scattered with sweaty middle-aged beautiful women in their bras and panties. I say middle-aged as a compliment, by the way. Everyone looks good at twenty, but if you are rocking a hot bod in your thirties and forties, then you're doing something. Yoga had officially been bumped above line dancing on my list of enjoyable recreational activities. Wishing I'd worn tighter underwear, I was glaringly ready to join this flexibility cult, and curious why my wife had sent me to sex camp.

Then the Calvin Klein male models disrobed, and the fantasy fell as flaccid as a Rosie O'Donnell reach around. Underneath, the dudes were wearing Speedos, and not the tight thick swimming ones either. They were wearing the thin chamois-like ones—loincloths, basically. Where do you even buy those? I've never seen them in my L.L. Bean catalog—I know that. How far does society have to crumble before grown men think it is acceptable to go to the gym in loincloths? Maybe if Armageddon were upon us, but in that case these men would surely be made into hushpuppies.

In my defense, I did last almost thirty minutes. Sweat was dripping from my nose as I unsuccessfully tried to reach my toes. As instructed, I then rocked back into a cobra-like pose, as did my cohorts. I had not chosen my mat location wisely. The man in front of me was clad in a bright yellow loincloth, which now, due to his excessive testicle sweat, looked like two tins of raw spam wrapped in saran wrap.

The man was well endowed, but not in the traditional way; I judged him to be somewhat average in the pepper grinder department. The beast that was staring at me was about as easy to ignore as a nail gun in my belly button. The Pangaea that was this man's scrotum was clearly losing its battle with continental drift. It looked like Jabba the Hutt's ball sack in a hot tub, and seemed painful, especially as he went into a lunge. On the next cobra stretch, I was staring directly between his continental plates, his third eye winking at me like a perverted pirate.

Check, please! Wet t-shirt show be damned, a heterosexual man can only look at so many balls and sphincters on a Tuesday afternoon.

"My wife's in labor," I lied to the skinny running the front desk.

"I didn't know she was pregnant," the man excitedly commented as the door closed on him mid-sentence.

After driving well above the speed limit, I flew in the front door and straight to the shower like a rape victim.

"It was cool, wasn't it?" my wife asked as I toweled off.

"I think our definitions of 'cool' are a bit different," I responded coldly.

"What do you mean?" she asked innocently. Innocence and gullibility are two of her best traits, although the gullibility has faded after ten years of marriage.

"I saw a man's asshole …" I said through gritted teeth, letting her know this conversation was going to be short and never repeated to another living soul.

"Banana hammocks?"

"How'd you guess?"

"I was going to mention that to you; it's a bit odd."

"Ya think?"

I then went for a two-hour run, desperately trying to get my testosterone levels back within their normal operating range. Even more disturbing than my eyes unwillingly losing their virginity is the fact that the entire town considered this normal, and also refused to make fun of these circus freaks. After two or three failed ball-sack jokes, I was quickly labeled the conservative American who just doesn't "get it." Apparently you cannot make fun of a man doing anything that is perceived as holistic, even if he does have a two-foot long scrotum.

3

HIPPIE HYGIENE

Call me weird: I'd never considered sticking coffee up my ass. Yes, I've enjoyed the Canadian socialized healthcare, and I believe in marriage for everyone, caring for the environment, evolution, and other liberal heresies. But why must I also be open to sticking random objects in my orifices in the name of good health?

My wife and I had traveled to Nelson, British Columbia, a spectacular part of the world—wilderness, snow-capped mountains, and more white-man drum circles than you can shake a stick at. The village is quaint, with great bars, restaurants, shopping, and coffee shops, all supported by ample amounts of disposable income provided by a plant going by names such as Blue Truck, Buddha Haze, or Purple People Eater.

It was New Year's Eve, and the entire town had been blanketed in ten inches of picturesque white powder. Ready for a good party, we put on our nicest blue jeans, fleece jackets, and toques (aka toboggans or beanies). Like most New Year's parties, this one was destined to fall limp of the preconceived dreams romantic comedies have wrongly forced into our brains. No love affairs start at 11:59 pm, glitter does not fall, and Billy Crystal will not be proposing to you any time soon. Plus, Billy Crystal is sixty-eight now and if he tried to sweep you off your feet, he might break a hip.

The music was popping, and the low-hanging sheet-like fog gave the party a certain ambience. The room smelled of polypro B.O. mixed liberally with the hay bale the group had split pre-party. The crowd consisted of athletic types who, even under layers of clothes, patchouli, dreads, and beards, still looked hot.

"Coffee enemas are good for you," said the cute hippie girl who smelled of forest-green crayons, which was surprisingly sensual.

She had the slow talk and blank stare that only the self-righteous possess. This look is also displayed at tent revivals, environmental protests, hostels, and the vitamin aisle at Whole Foods. She was a self-proclaimed healer and alternative medicine counselor, the type of person whose self-worth is propped up by the fact that she thinks she knows the secret cure for cancer. And maybe she does—she did go to Facebook med school for eight years. It just seems to me that if it actually worked, it would just be called medicine, instead of alternative medicine, and Moon Shadow would be bathing in Benjamins (or technically, she'd be bathing in Bordens, as Robert Borden is on the Canadian 100 dollar bill).

"Who says?" I asked, accidentally initiating a personal hygiene debate with a hippie.

"It just is," she answered.

"You'll have to do better than that. And don't say you read it on the Internet."

"It's ancient. People have been detoxing this way for thousands of years." (Have you ever noticed that hippie health treatments are always ancient, yet somehow the current practitioners are still the vanguards of the movement?)

"Are you sure you don't mean they've been drinking it for thousands of years?"

"It rids your body of toxins and trapped fecal matter. I do it once a month and have never felt better."

"I do it every morning. But, call me weird, my people just drink coffee."

"You're like talking to George Bush."

Don't worry, I'm not about to launch into some random ill-placed political diatribe here. It is now in vogue to ruin a good joke, fishing trip, or even simply drinking a beer with your buddy by shoving random Tourette-like political opinions into unrelated topics. Personally, I find the act of talking about politics more depressing than the politics themselves. Boring people tend to use political sound bites as a conversational crutch because they have nothing of value to add to normal conversations. Kind of like nuns ranking dildos.

However, if I have to choose between sticking coffee up my ass or being seen as a George Bush supporter—pass me a flight suit and the Old Testament and I'll meet you at the Texas ranch.

"Okay, I'll hear you out," I said skeptically.

<Insert hippie nonsense here>, Moon Shadow retorted.

"Do you let it cool first?"

"Of course," she said, as if that was the stupidest question she'd ever heard.

"It would take a pretty talented sphincter to sip it out of a cup."

"Funny ..."

"Dark or light roast?"

"Are you done yet?"

"Does it have to be black? I like cream and sugar."

"Do you have a head injury or something?"

"In all seriousness, do the organic and fair-trade ideals still apply?"

Moon Shadow stared at me through gritted teeth.

"Fair trade or not, it seems disrespectful to those hard working farmers." I was on a roll.

"Done?"

"I bet Juan Valdez is pissed."

"Done?!" she yelled loud enough for my wife to hear.

"Yes," I said after wracking my brain for other anal coffee jokes.

My wife closed in fast in the hope of salvaging her own hippie street cred.

"You're really enjoying this, aren't you?" she whispered in a way that left me wondering if she thought I was intelligently witty or regretted having children with me.

"Yes. And the Blue Truck doesn't hurt. That girl was telling me I should stick coffee up my ass," I grinned.

"Well …"

"Not you too?"

"It has some health benefits."

"Am I the only one here who's not high?"

"You are high."

"You know what I mean. I'm not sticking coffee up my ass; that's just irresponsible."

My wife smiled, letting me know I'm not alone on this planet, or at least that I amuse her. "Maybe you should go listen to that white Rasta over there," she told me in a low voice.

"Huh?"

"It involves urine."

"I'm on my way."

I arrived at the scene of the crime trying to hide my excitement. The conversation was identical to the coffee enema argument, but this time the group was discussing the merits of, among other things, drinking one's urine. (There is also a movement where men eat their own semen, but I'm trying my best to keep this thing PG-13.)

"It's full of vitamins and minerals your body was unable to absorb the first time," the man with the bug-infested white-man dreads said.

"Kind of like Gatorade," I interjected, showing my support for the cause.

"Exactly. It's completely natural and pure."

"Do you drink other people's urine?" I asked with a straight face.

"Don't be silly," he said. "That's disgusting."

So apparently, one man's waste product is another man's health smoothie. They even urinate on bandages and wrap sore joints to cure aches and pains. I guess they haven't heard of ibuprofen, as it not only cures the same ailment, it also has the added benefit of not smelling like a truck stop bathroom. I almost felt obligated to start a cult with these gullible snow people: solid money, great sex, and tons of weed. What's not to like?

If I do start a cult, I will have a strict bathing policy. Many of these mountain people do not use normal deodorant; they rub a magic crystal under their arms, which I guess is no stranger than rubbing a penis-shaped plastic container filled with white goo under your arm. However, *Webster* defines the word deodorant as: an agent for destroying odors. Most people who use the magic crystal smell like Janis Joplin's taint, so it's clearly not fitting the traditional definition of deodorant. To each his own: just don't expect me to spot you when you're doing squat-thrusts.

Trying to blend in, I quietly went and stood next to my wife. My wife is now a midwife (as well as a witch in the U.S.), and she was deep in a conversation with a local midwife about ways to encourage babies to slide on into life. As a midwife, my wife sees vaginas at their most scientific level. Personally, I like to take a more artistic view of this female body part, and not delve into the science of it. Kind of like eating a chili cheese slaw dog at the Varsity—just eat it, enjoy yourself, and get stoked for the game: don't go reading the nutritional information and ruin a good time.

This one conversation between two midwives has led to a ten-year argument between my wife and me about something fundamental: what is funny, and what is not funny.

On one side, you have my wife, a practical, logical woman who is one of the most likeable and lovely people on the planet. And then, you have me. My personality is more like puppet sex; you're either in the small minority that is really into it or, more than likely, you think it should be outlawed. To me, it's Never Leave A Joke Behind.

My wife quit laughing at my jokes over a decade ago, but that doesn't mean I don't keep trying. When it comes to telling awkward, inappropriate jokes at dinner parties, I've got the endurance of Lance Armstrong on meth. But there is only one joke she still laughs at: Spandex. I'm just a few ounces over the two-hundred-pound weight limit on Spandex (read the fine-print on the tag). But over the limit is still over. My body is just not the type that looks good crammed into a sausage casing. I do own a pair that I wear under my shorts when I'm spear fishing, in order to protect my boys against salt water chafing and lobster spines. But every so often, after a year or two of my wife answering my best hooks with a straight face, I will be forced to break out this fashion catastrophe.

"I'm going for a swim," I'll say, strutting into the room leaving nothing to the imagination.

"Not in those you're not," she'll say, busting into fits of laughter.

Every time, it kills. It's a humiliating way to get a laugh.

But I'll take it.

The only other thing my wife will laugh at is my ongoing fight with Phillip. Phillip is my archenemy. I hate this man. I belittle him with insults daily. He is sleeping with my wife. He also happens to be fictitious.

Originally, my wife's second, fictitious, husband was named Trevor until I had a friend named Trevor who was a 225-pound welder from Alberta, so we then moved to Preston. But then I knew a professional boxer named Preston, so now he's officially Phillip.

After my wife left me, she had to settle for a lesser man, or at least that's the way I tell it. Phillip comes up in conversation regularly around the house. Phillip is a pretty man and has perfect, flawless skin. He's overly enthusiastic about yoga, rarely cusses, doesn't have to shave that often, and is 5'9½" tall. He's really strong in a pound for pound kind of way, but not in a pound versus pound kind of way. Some women, especially those who live in cities, wouldn't know any better and would actually consider him quite the catch.

"You know Phillip doesn't cook breakfast every morning. He just eats chia seeds."

"You know Phillip pays someone to split his wood?"

"I bet Phillip couldn't open this jar of pickles."

"I bet Phillip would call an exterminator to kill the mice under the house."

"It would take Phillip three trips to carry all your luggage."

"I bet Phillip cries during romantic comedies."

"Whatcha wanna bet Phillip can't even fish?"

I'd be a horrible ex-husband. I would threaten, humiliate, and beat poor Phillip like a red-headed rented mule.

Which brings us back to our ongoing argument about what is funny and what is not. Being a self-proclaimed professional smartass, I feel I outrank her in judging humor. But, I'm usually wrong about most things. In my mind, jokes supersede everything: good taste, political correctness, and even reality. If a comedian says, "So I was on a plane on the way here," it doesn't have to be true. It's merely the setup of a joke, and therefore storytelling, and under the freedom of laughter amendment in our constitution, okay to lie about.

For example, I make one joke in this book about prostitutes, which my wife thinks we cut. She is 100-percent correct: prostitution is a horrible thing on so many levels, and in her moral, decent world, something that should never be joked about. This is where we disagree. If the joke is funny, it's funny. I don't mean that I literally have a prostitute in my kitchen, or that I want to put a hot pocket in her. I mean it figuratively. In fact, I don't even mean it figuratively; it is merely a setup for a hot pocket, microwave joke. Johnny Cash did not kill a man in Reno and Bob Marley might have communed with three little birds, but did not actually shoot a Sheriff (and obviously never a deputy).

According to my wife, and other civilized people, childbirth, yoga, women, and everything 'holistic' have this get out of jail free card when it comes to making fun of them. They can be as ridiculous as they want and never worry about ridicule; they just levitate above the rest of us immoral low lives.

So the conversation between these two midwives at the New Year's party provided what I thought was comic gold. The childbirth joke in question revolves around a woman having her first child in an unnamed hippie village in Canada. The baby was having a hard time coming out. And apparently, to help a baby down the water-slide to life, there are a few things you can do. You might have heard that climbing stairs, drinking castor oil, or even having sex can help (although the latter is like trying to dock an X-wing fighter to the Hindenburg). But apparently, nipple stimulation also works.

Now, I'm not denying the science behind this, as it is safe to assume, with a four-year degree in childbirth, my wife knows more about this subject. And, I watched *Old School* for the tenth time during the birth of our last child. And, okay, tough times call for tough measures, and I could see a husband trying to help his wife out if she were in dire pain.

But in this specific case, the man begins sucking his wife's nipples in front of: two midwives, one student midwife, his wife's mother, two dogs, two cats, and a ferret. Now, I think it actually did work, but that is not the question. The real question is whether or not we can make fun of him for starring in low-budget, low-quality, bloated hippie porn?

Most decent people go off on some worthless tirade about the miracle of life, blah, blah, blah, and miss the big picture. A man sucking his wife's nipples in front of four people and five animals is odd—I don't care what the context is. And this is the backbone of my argument with my wife, who is decidedly on the "never make fun of anything dealing with childbirth no matter how funny it is" wagon.

I'm not saying it doesn't work, I'm not saying childbirth is not beautiful (it's not, by the way), and I'm not even saying hippies are bad people. I'm just saying that a man sucking his wife's nipples in front of an audience is out of the ordinary enough that we should at least be able to call attention to the oddity and maybe have a few chuckles at his expense.

My wife reluctantly concedes that I've earned the right to make fun of this ridiculous, voyeuristic, overly hairy couple, but you will not catch her laughing at any nipple-sucking birth jokes anytime soon. Tough crowd.

Our vacation in the winter wonderland came to an end, and we did the white-knuckled eighteen-hour drive back home via the longest luge track in the world. This was down the infamous Highway 1, brought to international fame by *South Park*'s "Follow the Only Road" parody.

As we were detoxing from our trip to Hippie Disneyland, it was clear my wife's withdrawals would be worse than mine. The next day, I'm brushing my teeth when right there on the back of the toilet is something that left me bewildered and worried: organic tampons.

This was very confusing to me. Why were they organic? Was there a new hygiene trend that we needed to discuss as a society? Like vaccines, I think we just need to slow down a bit before we start making decisions that might impact society as a whole. This is not something to just rush into. Did this mean women are now going vegan, you know, down there? A move toward vegan vaginas could destroy civilization as we know it.

Was I now going to have to go out and get a tofu penis? I have to be honest with you, that just does not sound that enjoyable to me. Call me old fashioned, but I like a nice firm piece of meat. A tofu penis? That would be like getting a gynecological exam by one of the Muppets. And, I don't know about you ladies, but the idea of Kermit the Frog laying coals on me doesn't arouse me in the slightest. I mean, it might work for Miss Piggy, but hell, she is a two-foot-tall puppet. Or maybe I'm completely off base on this one.

4

PHALLIC DELIGHT

After seven years in Canada, I've become numb to the everyday shenanigans these ice fishing fools try to pass off as normal. It's nice to have a reality check every couple of years, and my family from Georgia provides just that. Without them, I might start to believe it's normal for a woman to take a dump with the door open (all Canadian women leave the door open: Céline Dion, Sarah McLaughlin, even the Bare Naked Ladies. And yes, I know Céline Dion is an alien and technically doesn't count.)

If you've read my first book you understand my mom is borderline saintly. She is now the most scrumptious grandparent you can imagine, and my brother, sister, and I fight over who gets to have her. As a public school teacher, and with three of us in college, world traveling was not really an option for my mom. For the most part, she hasn't left The South her entire life.

On one occasion, my mom came to Canada with my sister Marla and our Uncle Jesse (no relation to the Dukes). Uncle Jesse is from Fairhope, Alabama, and is a bachelor who never had kids. There would be rumors about his sexuality if not for the fact that ole Jesse is, and always has been, a drunken womanizer. Uncle Jesse is an honest, nice, drunken womanizer, so everybody loves having him around—he's highly entertaining. Watching a sixty-year-old man work his Southern swerve on Canadian seniors is worth the price of admission. Whenever he's on the prowl, he'll always change out of his overalls and into his one nice pair of slacks, topped with a crisp white button-up shirt. Those pants have got to be thirty years old, I remember him wearing them when he was hitting on one of the moms at my ten-year-old birthday party. Either that, or he bought a few dozen pairs back in the late '70s. Having never had kids, he thinks of us as his kids, and our kids as his grandkids. And like most Southerners, he also has barely left The South his entire life.

Uncle Jesse traveled during the Vietnam war with the army, but as most military men will tell you, jumping out of a plane with a parachute (glorified falling) with an M16 strapped to your chest is not exactly the same as kicking it in a youth hostel in Thailand playing Jenga. Now with my own family moving around like a band of gypsies, it gives Uncle Jessie an excuse to see some new parts of the world and hopefully keep me from drinking the Flavor Aid. (Little known fact: the Jonestown mass suicide victims did not actually 'drink the Kool-Aid' as the cliché would suggest. Kool-Aid is upbeat and cheerful, with a Grimace-like mascot; they needed something a little more budget, depressing, and bleak.)

Canada is spectacular in the summer, especially the west coast: whale watching, sailing, fishing, hiking, trapping beavers, clubbing seals—what's not to like? Like every other time they visited, my family stepped off the plane and took in a deep easy breath. Their last gulp of fresh air had been in rural Georgia in August, which is kind of like being in a sauna while an elephant urinates on the rocks. The next day I took everyone on a coastal hike around Victoria. Bald eagles flew overhead as waves crashed on the pebbled beach, and the giant trees surrounded by flowers gave us the feeling we were breathing in some top-shelf oxygen. After giving up hope on an eagle snatching one of the Chihuahuas from the beach (which they were known to do), we proceeded to the summer fair. We split up, my mom more into crafts, and my sister and I more into the edibles.

The fair was a large event. There was a band, jugglers, and hundreds of stalls selling a variety of hemp products and canned foods nobody could afford. Tables decorated with wagon wheels and washboards displayed gorgeous $15 loaves of bread, which, I can only guess, were stuffed with golden tickets at that price. The place was packed, and the heavy smoke from the gluten-free doughnut stand hovered over the crowd. I tend to be too cheap to buy anything, but there was one treat I always splurged on: chocolate-covered frozen banana.

Although delicious, and almost affordable, there is a dark side to this tasty treat. I handed the cute girl, who was actually rocking her white-girl dreads, a ten-dollar bill. From deep in her freezer, she then produced two of the largest, blackest, hardest, most phallic treats on the planet. I sheepishly handed one to my sister. In an effort to avoid a public deep-throating display we both simultaneously attempted to bite the tip off our midnight rockets. Nothing. We regrouped, inspected our teeth, and mounted a counterattack. Like beavers, we each gnawed at our foe like a giant frozen redwood tree. With our numbed mouths, drool ran down the shaft of our summer delicacy. It was no use. They were impenetrable.

At this point, we were both trying to contain our laughter to avoid drawing further attention to ourselves. Try sucking on a rock-hard frozen manlike treat without a smile on your face. Try it with your sister. My sister's head was on a swivel, trying to avoid an embarrassing run-in with Southern debutantes or maybe the paparazzi. She relaxed after I reminded her she only knew two people in Canada, and I was one of them.

"Why don't we head over to Fourth," I said, motioning my sister off Main.

"Right behind you."

Away from the main thoroughfare, we now enjoyed our frozen treats in privacy. It took us both about twenty minutes to chop our pornographic sweetness down to size. Wiping the chocolate from our faces, we did the walk of shame back to Main. We were now in the activist section of the fair. The booths tackled issues like global warming, pollution, and the ever present legalizing weed campaign. There was also a large gathering around the University of Victoria's rabbit-themed tent, which is where we met back up with a confused Uncle Jesse.

As far back as anyone can remember, everyone on my dad's side of the family has been a rabbit hunter; it's on their family crest along with kudzu and moonshine. The photos on the placard were not of the grey wild rabbits my uncle was accustomed to blowing away with a shotgun, but rather of cute, multi-colored bunnies, the kind that crap all over your house, reminding you how much of an idiot you were for getting your kids a pet to celebrate Christ rising from the grave.

"Is there a big hunt coming up?" Uncle Jesse asked, hoping he might squeeze in a Canadian rabbit expedition while he was up.

"Not exactly. It's a symposium."

"What's a symposium?"

"A meeting where nothing gets done."

"I've heard of those."

"Why don't you go check it out and get back to me?"

The University of Victoria had a real rabbit epidemic on its hands. Irresponsible students released their pet bunnies on campus after realizing it took too much effort to clean their bongs and take care of a pet at the same time. Rabbits, living up to their slutty reputation, soon overran the campus. The bunnies were destroying the expensive landscaping, covering the entire campus in doodoo pellets, and leaving bloodstains on the grass once the hawks and eagles discovered this Pez dispenser of tender meat. They even began to attract cougars, which wanted to make thigh-high boots out of them.

The issue: how do you get rid of a harmful, invasive species that is cute? Had they been rats or opossums, this would have been a much simpler matter. The anthropomorphism of animals is quite common. The reason I say this is because I enjoy obnoxiously squeezing large words into sentences to make myself appear smarter than I actually am.

My uncle squinted his face in disbelief as he read each of the tri-fold presentation boards closely. The proposals ranged from the expected cage traps to the extreme—a plan to shoot the bunnies with tranquillizer guns and subsequently neuter the lifeless fur balls. The tranquillizer proposal was getting most of the votes, and with its $80,000 price tag, had my uncle's attention.

With a serious, confused look on his face, Uncle Jesse strolled back over.

"What do ya think?" I asked, smiling.

"Nathan ..." Uncle Jesse looked serious. "Do Canadians not know how to kill rabbits?"

"Apparently not," I laughed. It should be noted, like a lot of older men, my uncle is only funny when he is not trying to be.

"They're gonna spend eighty grand to kill a few hundred bunnies. Hell, that's over two hundred dollars a rabbit!" Uncle Jesse said, sensing a moneymaking opportunity. "Do they not have twenty-twos in Canada?"

"Yeah, they got'm."

"Do they not know how to use them?"

"Well, no one at UVic anyway."

"Hell, me, you, and Brian could knock out this pandemic, as they call it, in one night. I'd be happy with a quarter of that eighty grand. How about you?" Uncle Jesse asked with a smile.

"I reckon a couple of bricks should do it," I answered (a brick is 500 rounds of twenty-two caliber bullets, in case you're from Canada or shop at The Gap).

"We might need some Michelobs, maybe a thermos of coffee, if they want us to do it at night."

"Yeah. Those Maglites too, the ones you duct tape to the barrels. Maybe a potato silencer if they want us to be discrete," I added. "Hell, it sounds like fun. Should I go tell them we'll do it for free if they throw in the Michelobs?"

"Sure thing, I'm in!" Uncle Jesse answered as we walked away from the thought-provoking debate on how to kill a bunny.

If you must know, half the rabbits were shipped to Texas, where unbeknownst to the administration at UVic they were used to teach rifling skills to grade three students in a small suburb outside Houston. The other half were sent to a hobby farm four hours away where they quickly escaped onto the neighbor's real farm, which came with a real farmer, with a real shotgun, and he ended the other half of the epidemic in thirty minutes or so. The University of Victoria now has a severe grass problem on their hands. Let's hope this bastion of higher learning will be able to solve this conundrum before it's too late.

"You know they have an American bullfrog problem, too," I offered.

"What's an American bullfrog?"

"Just a bullfrog. But because it's fat and invasive, it makes Canadians feel good about themselves to call it American. They're trying the same tranq gun idea."

"Damn. I didn't know they made darts that small. No gigs, huh?"

"Nope."

We were still laughing about the bunny and frog epidemic when we ran back into my mom. She had carefully selected a few pottery mugs and a bar of chocolate. My mom was in her element. Had it not been for two very large twins in her belly, she would have never given up her hemp necklace enterprise back in the seventies.

"You guys want some of this chocolate bar?" my mom offered.

"Uh … no," I said, hoping this conversation would not go any further and we could keep our summer indiscretions a secret.

"Suit yourself. The girl who sold it acted as if it were gold."

She bit into her delicious hippie treat. It barely made it past her teeth before she started gagging and spitting the nonsense on the ground.

"How do you fuck up chocolate?" my mom said, shocked. My mom never cusses, and when she does it's hilarious. It's ironic, because my brother, sister, and I can talk in only four letter words for months.

"What is it?" I asked.

"Well, it sure as hell ain't chocolate. This shit cost me seven bucks." She was on a roll. I explained the substance in question was carob, a chocolate alternative.

"Why would you substitute chocolate in the first place? It says it right here on the label. Chocolate bar. Shouldn't a chocolate bar have chocolate in it? It sure as hell doesn't say anything about, 'may contain tree bark.'"

On the way home, we took a detour to TCBY to cleanse my mom's palate with some frozen yogurt. My sister and I were not quite ready for anything frozen. We briefed my mom on the rabbit situation.

"Do Canadians not know how to kill rabbits?" she asked.

Don't let the pottery mugs fool you; my mom grew up on a farm in Selma, Alabama, and happens to be a real gun hand (even though she will deny it to appear classier and more civilized than the rest of us).

"It is great to have you guys up," I answered. Any risk of me being Canadianized was crushed for a few more years.

5

CARNIES MAKE GREAT BABYSITTERS

My wife and I are now taking applications to add another wife or husband to our family. We desperately need to bring a little reason and maturity to our relationship. We need adult supervision. Our family of four has now relocated to a remote town in Canada's northern Yukon (think Alaska).

Everyone asks, "How did you end up in the Yukon?" The same way we ended up in our other three countries and six homes.

"I love the Yukon," I might say, looking at a map. "Great fishing."

"Me, too," my wife answers.

"We should go there," I casually respond.

"I'll do it," my wife says, trying to establish spontaneity dominance.

"No, you won't."

"Yes, I will!"

"I'll do it!" I might call back, my Southern do-not-dare-me pride kicking in.

"No you won't."

It is like listening to two ten-year-old Southern boys daring each other to derail a train. And the next thing you know, you've got moose coming out of your ass. No, not literally.

In a husband, we are looking for a bald, pot-bellied man who is handy with a skill saw, able to tie flies, and most importantly, has no sense of humor. The would-be wife must also be homely. A naïve man might expect me to ask for a twenty-four-year-old Swedish swimmer, but let's be realistic here, this is not *Penthouse Letters*. I've got a family to think about. Our second wife must laugh at all my jokes and stupid stories, no matter how many times she has heard them, and if she can fillet fish and handle international accounting that would be a plus.

As a new Canadian, I have yet to learn how to take care of alabaster white skin and with the twenty-four-hour sunlight and killer fly-fishing, I was guaranteed a Dante's *Inferno* level sunburn the second our plane landed. Due to an unfortunate infected pierced labia joke, it took us longer to settle into our new town than we had expected. After a week in our new house (whose owners actually enjoyed the pierced labia joke) we were somewhat back into a routine.

Our small town of 5,000 people had ballooned to 20,000 for the two-day A & P Show (Agricultural and Pastoral). Cows, sheep, dog trials, it was so Canadian I was expecting a Sasquatch to steal my corndog at any time. FYI: a corndog in the Yukon is still called a corndog, but if you order a hotdog, you'll get a premium homemade battered corndog. This is advanced civilization at its best.

At the fairgrounds, the Yukon farmers led their prized steers and sheep through the crowds, allowing the animals to socialize with the masses and eat cotton candy before sending them back to a life of eating briars and wallowing in shit for the other 364 days of the year. Yukon farmers could give a pile of sheep shit as to how the rest of the world has been dressing for the last thirty years.

I thought it impossible, but somehow, some way, a Yukon rancher can sport a sweater-vest and actually make it look manly. They are also German immigrant Yukon ranchers who rock short-shorts like they are cruising South Beach. They leave little to the imagination, and I have to admit, they also make this fashion Molotov cocktail look normal. These sleeves of fabric are not only worn socially, but are also standard issue work wear. It seems unhygienic. My wife has been begging me to buy a pair, but I remain hesitant; her motives are unclear.

As my family's designated Life Sherpa, I was carrying all of our food, drinks, and clothing along with my two-year-old son. As I was checking out a new El Camino (!), my son planked out with every muscle in his body flexed beyond comfort. I thought the usual.

"Poo?" I whispered in his ear.

All I got back was slack-jawed silence.

"Are you okay, little man?"

Although speechless, he slowly raised one arm and pointed toward the horizon. "Cathel," was all he could get out.

I am not the most intuitive parent, and most of the time it takes me weeks to figure out what a toddler actually wants, but even I could figure this one out. Taking up half the horizon was the largest blowup castle in the northern hemisphere. Actually, to call it a castle is a bit of an insult; it was more of a blowup metropolitan area. Scattered across the landscape were rows of blowup tunnels large enough to drive my 1992 Subaru Impreza through (being a professional smartass is not as lucrative as one might guess). These subway tunnels connected the larger blowup castles, mountains, climbing walls, pizzerias, and payday loan offices within the giant complex. It was the Death Star, and every kid within fifty miles was stuck in the tractor beam.

I was relieved to see the giant spray-painted *$5 A KID* sign tacked crookedly to a spindly pine-tree. This was the best deal I had found since the chocolate covered phallic delight. Almost all Yukoners still subscribe to a hands-off style of parenting, similar to how I was raised back in the '80s. But when it comes to free-range parenting, only one person reigns supreme.

When we finally made it to the front of the line, there was God's gift to childcare: Yukon Joe Dirt. I later found out Joe was a lifer carnie, and his parents had been proudly operating the Zipper for the last thirty-eight years. His feathered rattail flapped in the gentle breeze like a mud flap on a moped. Joe was too cool or hot to button more than two buttons of his sleeveless flannel shirt.

"That'll be ten bucks, bro," Joe said to me, the removal of

the hand-rolled cigarette from his mouth not even an option as he stuffed his jean shorts with sweaty five-dollar bills.

"This seems like the place to be," I complimented Joe.

"Sweet as," he answered, obviously proud of his entrepreneurial endeavor.

"How long can they stay?"

"All day, bro. We close at six."

"I guess I'll just leave them here and go get a beer with my wife," I joked as my two and five year olds sprinted for the pugil sticks, which were being used as bats to hit the required battle helmets over the fence.

"Yeah, no prob," Joe answered, turning to get his next stack of fives.

"Want to get lunch?" I asked my wife.

"We can't leave them here. Hank's two," my wife answered, pointing out the obvious.

"He seems responsible enough," I said, nodding toward Joe.

My wife just smiled as Joe began rolling another smoke (this despite the fact he was a strict mouth breather and still puffing away on the one in his mouth). We couldn't leave them, but it was tough to turn down such a deal.

A light rain had started, and I bought us two coffees to celebrate a four-and-half-minute date with my wife under a tree.

"Where are they?" I asked my wife when I returned.

"I'm not sure. They might be on the back of the mountain."

Blowup Everest was located on the fifty-meter line (54.7-yard line) of the rugby field. Joe must have had a 747 engine keeping this thing inflated.

"Dada!" my older son yelled from the peak. As I looked up, he commenced sliding down the north face, which was now a giant Slip n' Slide. He reached me with a huge smile, Velcro scratches, and some kind of festival grime I could not readily identify.

"Where's Hank?" I asked.

"I'm not sure."

"You're his big brother, and he follows you everywhere. You have to look out for him."

"He might be on the mountain."

We then looked up to see wild man Hank crouched at the top of Mt. Everest.

"Poo," is all we could make out through all the yelling and generators.

My wife looked at me in horror.

"Hey, you're the climber, not me," I answered, not even waiting on the question.

"It's not a real mountain," she answered, rolling her eyes.

"You're an athlete," I said, hoping positive encouragement would help.

"I hate you," she answered, sitting her coffee down.

My wife then began a hilarious ascent of an ass-slick fifty-foot-tall plastic mountain to retrieve her doodoo-packed piñata from the peak. My older son and I sat and watched the spectacle. Luckily she found a seam and was able to chimney (climbing lingo, potentially used incorrectly) up for the rescue. With the caca basket in hand she slid down the grimy waterslide and impressively stuck the landing.

"If you drank my coffee, I'm punching you in the mouth," she growled as she squeegeed the slime from her jeans.

This would have been an optimum time to have our second husband/minion. I believe a mutual hatred of a completely incompetent second husband might actually strengthen a marriage. We could team up and treat the poor boy like a rented mule.

Please email your resume with photo and a sample of your fly-tying to: Nathan@NathanWeathington.com

6

THE STAY-AT-HOME DAD EXPERIMENT

When my two sons were two and four, my wife convinced me that it would be a good idea for me to become a stay-at-home dad while she went back to school in a town an hour north of Victoria. My wife would also be out of town for fifteen weeks a year during this period, leaving me alone and outnumbered. She's a helluva of salesman is all I can say, and showing me videos of steelhead slurping dry flies on YouTube was just playing dirty pool in my opinion. She also convinced me it would be a good idea for me to quit my high-paying job to focus on being a writer, this despite the fact I'm barely qualified to send a text. Keep in mind you make about as much money selling a book as a snow cone. Just to be clear, I mean an actual snow cone, shaved ice with artificial flavor, not the sex act (which pays considerably more than selling a book).

The one thing I can say with absolute certainty about the stay-at-home dad experiment is that sweatpants are way more comfortable than a suit. You can quote me on that. When I told people I was a stay-at-home dad, I got varied responses. Most of the men discounted me as a worthless flake. Luckily, I'm at the point in my career(s) where I don't have to worry about what other men think of me, which is why I was able to get away with wearing Crocs in public. My sons and I just smugly sipped our Capri Suns in the driveway as these real men drove away to their cubicles of fulfillment.

Women, on the other hand, had more complex ideas about my stay-at-home dad status (as one might expect). Some were shocked, some thought we were a ball of cuteness, and others were more aggressive.

"It's so much harder than you thought it would be, isn't it?"

I wasn't sure if this was a question. And if it was a question, I had the sense there was a right and wrong answer. I made the mistake once of being honest and answering, "No, not really." This woman opened up a can on me. She started yelling at me, telling me that I had no idea how difficult it was to be a stay-at-home mom, which I'm pretty sure was not the question she asked me.

What I mistook for small talk, it seems, was actually a highly charged political question. As a rookie playground attendee, I didn't realize that this was my cue to reaffirm how difficult her Ann-Taylor-dressed life was. She dressed like a woman who rarely laughs.

"When my husband's at work, it's like I'm a single mother!"

I found this disrespectful to actual single mothers. I guess she *was* a single mother, with two major caveats:

A) She had a husband.

B) Her husband was at work making mad cash for her to able to dress her little precious in Gucci clothes.

My wife was away for large parts of the year and not working. If anybody was a single mother it was me.

And what's with the heckling? What if I heckled women when they returned to work? "Welcome to the real world, bitch!" I'd rightfully be unemployed. Why must everything be the hardest thing in the world? Is there no second place? Or maybe forty-third?

When my boys were younger, my wife took care of them. I saw how hard she worked, so it honestly did not come as any surprise that I might have to skip a few winks to ensure everyone's ass got wiped. I'm not saying it was easy, but it's not the 'Most Difficult Job on the Planet' as we now love to call it. (Stop what you are doing right now and watch Bill Burr's bit about The Most Difficult Job on the Planet, or call me and I'll recite it for you.)

To be honest with you, it's harder to be a stay-at-home dad than a stay-at-home mom and it's still not the 'most difficult job on the planet' <cue gasp from the crowd>. Yeah, I said it, and my wife will back me up on this. Everything is the same except one tiny tidbit: it's lonelier. Moms can invite other moms home for coffee. The one dude in sweatpants at the sandbox cannot. It just doesn't sound right, especially in our small town where everyone was either already married or related. So a sober dude trying to make casual conversation to a stranger is obviously up to something. I always wanted to tell them that I wasn't hitting on them, that I was just lonely and needed someone to run some inappropriate jokes by. No matter how hard I tried, I always ended up hanging out with the same two minors, maybe cooking too many pancakes and cookies, but nobody in my camp ever seemed to mind. And at the end of the day, even if my boys had been dicks, at least I had been hanging out with people I loved all day, unlike Fred in accounting who smells like pickles.

Don't get me wrong, trying to earn a living while taking care of two boys left me very little me time; I barely had time to even enjoy a cup of coffee. My coffee would start off hot and black, but after countless interruptions by two small boys, it would be off colored and taste of ass, similar to Michael Jackson post *Thriller*.

And it seems everyone is stuck in a perpetual circle jerk, patting each other on the back proclaiming how hard we work, how hard 'our' people work. On every stop I made on my first book tour, middle-aged men repeatedly made small talk by telling me how hard they were working. Really? We're drinking lattes in Barnes and Noble on a Tuesday afternoon; you might not be wringing the bar towel as hard as you might think. People who do work hard don't actually say it: they're too damn tired to muster up such conversation fillers. These hard-working men looked to me to reciprocate the banter, but I just couldn't make myself say it with a straight face sipping Starbucks in my whoring jeans (brother's gotta do what a brother's gotta to do to sell books). My grandfather worked hard. I do not, and my candy-ass hands are a dead giveaway. I'm okay with that and it would be disrespectful to my elders to say otherwise. Even my publisher fell for the trend.

"We don't want to book you too many straight days—you're gonna get tired," Ben said over the phone.

"Hey Ben, I'm away from my kids and selling shit jokes in air-conditioned bookstores that give me free coffee all day."

"Good point. I'll book you solid," he answered.

Are we nostalgic for when things were hard? I enjoy reading *Grapes of Wrath*, but I have no desire to live it. And where does hard work actually get you? You can dig a ditch as hard as you can go all day, but you still just have a ditch at the end of the day; you do not have an iPhone. Is it because we no longer have any real suffering in our lives? Nothing I do is the hardest thing in the world.

At the playground, I did want to blend in better, so I started agreeing with other women when they told me how difficult their lives were, as they played pity poker with their rivals. I am not saying that there are not real issues around gender equality, but maybe we could tone it back just a wee bit. You're driving up in your Land Rover and telling me how hard it is to be a rich white woman in the western world. I feel ya, girl. The Struggle is real.

Once the ladies at the sandbox saw that I was not going to have a nervous breakdown, their comments evolved.

"It must be nice to be fishing with your boys all the time."

Wait ... What happened there? I thought I was doing the

most difficult job on the planet?

"Your poor wife, it must be hard for her being away at school."

Uh ... she's in college—you know, coffee shops, deep conversations, smokin' grass, college. (Do they still call it grass?) Are you trying to tell me my wife is now doing the most difficult job on the planet again? How'd that happen? I'm now working from home, making all our money, taking care of the kids, the house, all the cooking, while my wife is out of town reading books, and we're worried about her workload?

For the record, my wife never said this nonsense. Well, maybe she did once after she had more than the daily recommended allowance of feminist classes. She was mad that I didn't clean the house as much as her. I quickly pointed out that she was correct; she did and still does clean the house more than I do. I then challenged her to name one other thing she did for our family. She stared at me blankly for a few long seconds and we then hugged it out and it's never been brought up again.

I think there is this misconception that men love going to work. Work kind of blows. You're hanging out with people for years that you don't even care about. If they die, you feign sadness, but deep down you know you're still going to Netflix binge that night as if nothing happened. If a woman wants to run Coca-Cola or IBM, go for it, I'm right behind you, I hate old white dudes. But be careful you're not trading away homemade popsicles for Venn diagrams.

To run a successful man camp, the first thing we realized was that we were going to have to ignore a lot of society's rules.

My kids were not signed up for endless classes after school, and on many occasions they did not even attend school at all. This left us free for other important projects, such as installing a blow-up castle in my kid's bedroom. At one point, I did receive an "excessive days away from school" complaint from one of the teachers.

"What did he miss in today's class?" I asked the teacher.

"We're studying fish right now."

"He caught and dissected twenty salmon yesterday, and read *Old Man and the Sea* last night. I think he'll be okay."

"Oh," was all she could say.

On another occasion, as I was signing my son back into school, the receptionist asked why he had been absent.

"The damsel fly hatch was on—it's a holiday we observe every year," I answered.

"Excuse me?"

"Yeah, the hatch was on," my son reiterated to try and further clarify the situation.

This later turned into an important life lesson for my boys. One day, we took the largest salmon from our cooler, with a street value of over $300, and wedged it into the teachers' lounge refrigerator. We have not had an excessive-days-away-from-school complaint since.

My kids are also allowed to stay in the car by themselves. Even on hot days! A panicked woman once ran up and opened the door to my car to save my kids from certain doom. They looked up from their books as if she was a crazy person trying to kidnap them. And to be expected, she also lambasted me for being an irresponsible parent for putting my kids in a deadly Easy Bake oven. I explained that my kids were quite advanced for their age, and will actually get out of the car when it gets too hot. They're quite gifted.

Our neighbor once yelled at me when my boys and I were up on the roof of our house cleaning out the gutters. I'm not sure why he was worried about my kids; they have better balance than I do, and if they fell they'd heal in a few minutes, where I'd be limping for years. It would be more appropriate to tell two little boys to get their dad off the roof.

I'm not one for doling out advice, but if you find yourself in a position where you have a choice between TPS Reports or watching Chip and Dale, pop some popcorn and quit overthinking everything, you moron.

7

NEVER GO FULL HIPPIE

My wife and I had been invited to a friend's hippie brunch. The word "hippie" was not expressly written on the invitation, but it was implied, as the directions included moveable objects (deer) and the words ethereal and sustainable. (Full disclosure: The deer were actually standing right where our host said, and we did in fact take a "hard left turn at the majestic buck."). It was a lovely autumn day and their property was surrounded by brightly colored trees. I find Autumn and Fall are very similar. Fall tends to coincide with football games while Autumn has something to do with apple harvesting.

Our friend's husband was the type of guy who hugs another man when they're first introduced. On top of this, he would do the very long, sanctimonious hippie hug, the one that in their minds makes them look more at one with the universe, but actually just makes straight men cringe and hold their breath until it's over—similar to having an orgy with the cast of *The View*.

There are two and only two reasons you should ever hug another grown man for an extended amount of time:

1. Winning a state championship;
2. Double-digit trout on a dry fly.

Other than that, you are embarrassing everyone in the room.

He's also the type of guy who thinks he's saving the world just by gracing us with his zen-like presence. Mind you, he's never actually done anything more than send links around Facebook or disdainfully question my diet, but in his mind, he's out running Habitat for Humanity. If your entire personality is based on the fact that you think you are better than other people, aren't you kind of by definition not very zen? He also has one of those good-looking heart-shaped faces, the kind that lets you get away with wearing designer hats or grooming stylish facial hair. As far as I'm concerned, unless you're making millions of dollars in a boy band, there is no reason to ever groom five o'clock shadow. So obviously I hated this good-looking ass-hat.

Our friends live in a yurt. Depending on how you look at it, a yurt is either a very portable, very cheap house, or, a very heavy, very expensive tent. It is about the size of an above ground swimming pool, and almost as useful. Why own a swimming pool you can't do a flying squirrel into? And, why own a house that makes the first of the three little pigs look like Frank Lloyd Wright?

Our friends are the type of folks who insist Ultimate Frisbee and Hacky Sack should be Olympic sports, and they also take composting *very* seriously. The benefits of compost, the ingredients, optimal temperature by layer, location, what type of bugs should live in there—it's endless. I do compost, but I don't give it much thought. Huck everything in a bin, and eventually it makes dirt (aka soil for you more sophisticated composters). And in the meantime, the compost bin is a great place to gather worms for fishing, which is really the only reason country boys do it. In The South, a bucket full of food scraps is called a slop-bucket, i.e. what you feed the pigs. It seems there is a fine line between a slop bucket and a compost bucket, and that line seems to run parallel to the Mason-Dixon line.

I was very excited for a real meal; I'd been suffering from an eating disorder brought on by a trip to Cirque du Soleil. If you ever really need to drop a few pounds before a class reunion, wedding, or pole-dancing class, I highly recommend this low-fat show of flying muscles. Before the second act, you will find yourself pinching your muffin top, wondering why you can't do a one-armed pull-up like the ninety-pound Chinese girl. You can achieve the same result by going to a YMCA men's dressing room and looking at nude eighty-year-old men. It took two weeks before I could keep any solid food down, and I haven't eaten a prune or rutabaga in over five years.

It was an impressive spread; these dirt fairies knew how to bake. Homemade biscuits, muffins, omelets, and some damn cinnamon rolls that would give you the Jimmy Leg. They were so good, I still feel guilty about writing this story. Our hosts were morally conscious earthlings and I'd already learned not to expect bacon at this type of shindig, but the homemade peach jam more than made up for the pork deprivation.

Our friend is a hardcore evangelical vegetarian, and I played along with her diatribe, and I even agreed with her hatred of salted country ham, which left me feeling uneasy, as if I'd just allowed someone to get away with insulting my grandmother. Eventually, though, I just couldn't sit through another PowerPoint explaining why she was a spiritual goddess and I'm just a colossal dung ball taking up valuable space on planet Earth.

There was even porridge at the brunch. Honest-to-God porridge. Not oatmeal, not grits, not Cream of Wheat, but full-on Three-Little-Bears porridge. I'd always thought it was a figure of speech or another word for oatmeal. It was actually pretty good with the virgin hand-picked berries, although I'm still unsure what porridge actually is. I'm also unsure about the virgin berries. Are they the first crop of berries from a new bush? Or, are they all picked by Tim Tebow?

My family tree involves several unidentifiable branches, and from this dubious racial background, everyone in my family has somehow evolved the stomachs of hobo goats. When I was a kid, as far as we were concerned, food poisoning or indigestion was just something Yankees and city people had to deal with. Now a Weathington stomach can handle anything, but maybe we've over-trained. My system is built to handle spicy pork rinds, pesticide-soaked okra, body shots of white-gravy, and government-issued five-gallon buckets of Neapolitan ice cream. At this delicious feast, I'd been pounding the hand-ground coffee (no kidding, they used an old pencil sharpener) along with the baked goods, and unfortunately, the organic porridge. This delicious hippie spread did not include sugar, poison, preservatives, any type of processed food, and not even a dollop of butter (still to this day referred to as a spice by my health-conscious mother). The brunch was just too damn wholesome and pure for my mutt-like stomach, and the porridge in the basement starting talking to me.

At first it was a subdued grumbling, like a light bass line from a Bee Gees song, but it quickly grew to Johnny Cash singing in a barrel. Stay calm, I told myself; don't panic, it's organic. I held out as long as possible. Normally, you'd retreat to the closest bathroom, blow the doors off, do a courtesy flush mid excavation, and maybe spray some potpourri around to cover your tracks. Still embarrassing, but not life altering. This is assuming of course your friends live in a house like normal human beings and not the hippie version of a singlewide.

At this point, the yurt was no longer an affordable, portable house; it was a tent. The tent was basically one small round room, sixteen feet in diameter, so no matter how much you excel at geometry, the bathroom is never more than four feet from your poached eggs. This seems unhygienic at the best of times, but at this particular juncture, it was downright hazardous. I looked outside first. There was very little cover, and the closest forest (the one with the majestic buck) was almost two hundred yards away.

Maybe I could make it.

No I couldn't.

Damn it.

Back inside.

The toilet, and I use the term loosely, was stationed behind a Japanese paper wall. Literally, a paper wall. Just to clarify, I do mean the actual word literally here, not the new hipster bastardized version of the word literally, which does not mean literally at all, but in fact means figuratively. This always makes me wonder why they chose the word literally to begin with. The English language is confusing enough as it is; why are we replacing words with other words with different meanings? This wordplay could create real havoc; we might start confusing rectal and oral thermometers, clapping versus the clap, or an oboe with a rusty trombone.

Johnny Cash was rolling around the bend just as I discretely ducked behind the origami wall. The toilet was a white porcelain seat sitting on top of a five-gallon bucket. A bucket! A goddamn bucket! These hippies were shitting in a bucket! Later I find out this was a composting toilet, which does sound better, but does not change the fact that you are taking a dump in a bucket like a refugee at a hunting camp. They actually compost their own caca and later add it to their tomato garden. I swore then and there that I'd never eat another veggie at my friend's house, which has been easy, as I've never been invited back.

I'll get as graphic as my Southern upbringing allows. It sounded like a cement mixer was laying a new section of I-20 in this poor family's tent. I reached back for the courtesy flush. No flush, you idiot, you're shitting in a bucket! A cold sweat rolled down my forehead as the brunch party inevitably went silent; nobody was even courteous enough to fake a loud GMO debate to help me save face.

After I washed my hands in the finger bowl, I came around the paper wall to find eight people avoiding eye contact with me; a reasonable move considering I'd just soiled their buffet.

"That was interesting," my wife said, as we got back into the car.

"I don't want to talk about it," I responded.

"You could have at least ..."

"I said I don't want to talk about it. Southerners do not talk about anything that happens in the bathroom."

"Well, it's not much of a bathroom."

"You've got me there. Who shits in a bucket?"

"It's a composting toilet. If we build a house, we should have one."

"Save it. I've heard the pitch. It's still crapping in a bucket. I'll back you on most of your Earth-saving endeavors, but not this one. I have to draw the line somewhere."

I've been invited to brunch elsewhere many times since this event. The hosts always seem surprised when on the RSVP I include two follow-up questions:

1. What can I bring?

2. Do you live in a yurt and/or shit in a bucket?

You don't have to be Bob Villa to know that if you're going to serve hand-ground coffee and organic porridge, your house is not up to code if you do not have a proper flushing toilet.

8

RIDING BAREBACK, BAREBACK

Some things should be left to the imagination. Things like hernia scars, birth marks on your rear end, the color of your prostate, or whether or not a 300-pound man has been circumcised.

It was mid-July and my wife and I, along with our two sons, were vacationing on one of British Columbia's spectacular hippie-infested Gulf Islands. After we explored the cute shops that sold hemp sandals and felt hats no one has worn in public since Jesus and Robin Hood, my wife insisted we go to "one of the best beaches in Canada."

As we approached the water, I had to give my wife credit; the white sand beaches, tidal pools, and rock formations made me feel like I was walking into a postcard.

And then ... the natives showed up, and besides a few anklets and toe rings, there was not a stitch of clothing to be seen on the entire beach. I'm not a total prude; this was not my first trip to a nude beach. I've even participated in the rare "I drank a handle of Wild Turkey on a Thursday" mishap. Therefore I did not hit the beach giggling like a fourteen-year-old Amish boy.

"I ain't takin' my clothes off," I whispered to my wife.

"Don't worry, me either," my more free-spirited wife replied.

We have a strict No Public Nudity policy with the kids or in front of guys Nathan plays poker with.

Many years before this, my wife and I had led a group of teachers over a sand dune in the Florida Keys where we stumbled across a very surprised nude couple. The man quickly retreated and dressed himself in a large-meshed thong-type apparatus. It looked like pink playdough that had been rolled in hair, being smushed through chicken wire. "How is that better?" my wife whispered in my ear.

To their credit, the Canadian island residents were more attractive than their Florida Keys counterparts, who all tend to be overweight guys with sunburnt penises—penises that always remind me of baby birds choking on pretzels. (FYI: My editor and I spent more time discussing the plural of penis than any other grammatical situation in this book.)

The first lady we approached was not unattractive, but not exactly Kate Winslet either. Her hair was greyish straw, pulled back in a French braid. She was heavyset, with skin the texture of a gorilla's hands and, to be expected, no tan lines. I salute her dedication to skin cancer—no easy task here in the rainiest place on earth. She was busy going to town on a large waffle cone of ice cream.

Maybe if it were only one scoop, maybe if it were vanilla instead of chocolate, maybe if she weren't deep-throating the cone down to the second scoop like she was trying to pay the rent, and maybe if I wasn't from Bremen, Georgia, then maybe, just maybe, I could have kept it together. I didn't. The floodgates opened, and I let go of five years of pent up hippie laughter I had buried away to help sustain my marriage. I flew into hysterics, unable to breathe, with barely audible laughter coming from my throat as tears flowed down my cheeks. My wife jerked me out of my hyperventilation fit with a sharp pinch on the back of my arm as she tugged me away from one very upset ice cream connoisseur.

Once we were a safe distance away from Debbie Does Double-Scoop, we cast our blanket with the regular nudists, the ones who simply tanned, read, and/or smoked weed. Eventually, I no longer noticed the female natives' beanless beanbags, and focused on my sons' sand castle.

Next up, Yoga Man, twelve o'clock: nude downward dog. You've got to be kidding me; I was now staring at this man's spleen from about five yards away.

"What's he doing, Dada?" my older son asked.

"Acting like a complete idiot, that's what," I answered, loud enough for Yoga Man to hear and hopefully remove his butthole from my line of sight, which I did not find nearly as humorous as someone deep-throating an ice cream cone. My wife slapped me on the chest. Now that I write this, it occurs to me that there is a lot of violence in our relationship. Yoga Man didn't flinch, and probably couldn't hear with all the blood rushing out of his anus and into his head. He did, however, change to a less vomit-inducing position, although I still consider a nude man doing wall sits to be abnormal and uncivilized family entertainment. Thirty minutes later, he tired and settled into his book on crystals.

I later tried making fun of this fool with my Canadian friends, who once again staunchly defended yoga as some type of all-knowing god never to be questioned, especially by an American. I am not questioning yoga or nudity, or even nude yoga in the privacy of your own home. However, I am questioning nude yoga performed by a worn out fifty-five-year-old ass-clown when he is closer to me than the beer cooler. My kids' pediatrician, my mechanic, and my plumber I fully trust and never question, but if I'm staring at their rectum while they change my spark plugs, I will question their behavior.

By the way, maybe try tipping your mechanic instead of Captain Ponytail who makes your coffee. I assure you that replacing a head gasket is more difficult and valuable than pouring hot water through coffee grounds. P.S. I'm also not calling you a barista; you make coffee, bring it down a notch.

There were other somewhat normal athletic activities all around—paddleball, bocce ball, Frisbee—all of which take very little actual effort or straining. Windsurfing does however require straining, and straining should never happen while nude, especially in public. I'm pretty sure they covered this on *Seinfeld*. This man was ruthless. The fact that there was zero wind did not deter our grunting, clinching friend, who balanced on his board, traveling considerably slower than the bocce ball across our field of vision. Keep in mind this is Canada, the water is cold, very cold, and Captain Windsurfer was not exactly show-ready.

"Wait until you see Lady Godiva," my friend and editor Jody mumbled from under her sunhat. Jody is a brilliant woman who is tasked with making my nonsensical, inappropriate jokes read like actual English, and the same person who had to put up with my peni vs. penises argument.

"Come on, don't leave me hanging," I answered.

"You'll just have to wait. But you might want to get your notepad out."

Two hours later, after lunch, I heard horse hooves coming down the trail.

"Are you sure you can handle this?" Jody asked.

"Handle what?" is all I got out as Lady Godiva came bursting through the trees. The horse was a stunning palomino, and the rider was a thin, buck-ass naked fifty-year-old woman torn from the centerfold of the AARP swimsuit edition. Her salt-and-pepper hair flowed behind her like a cape. Before retiring to a life of nude-hippiedom she'd been a stripper at a vegan strip club in Portland called *The Meatless Beaver*. Their slogan was "Our meat is on the pole, not on the plate." I am not making this up.

She still had the stripper hair, and her body was like Bourbon Street on a Sunday morning; you could tell it had recently been a lot of fun, but would now need dim lights and a fresh coat of bleach before it would draw a crowd. Not only was Lady Godiva bareback, she was also riding bareback. No saddle, no blanket, just the Big V pressed straight onto horsehair. Given the day's previous activities, this behavior almost seemed normal and hygienic, and I hate to admit it, but it was pretty hot.

"Wow," I said in a whisper, "I'm speechless."

"I thought you'd like that," Jody answered.

We then sat in silence, watching Lady Godiva gallop the horse along the beach and into the water, leaving Captain Windsurfer in her wake. She then stood on the horse's back, leaping into the ocean with a perfect jackknife. After remounting and squeezing the saltwater from her ageing stripper locks, she galloped back through the trees, never uttering a word to anyone, like Jodi Foster in *Nell*. No one on the beach flinched, further evidence that Canada is finally succumbing to the U.S. mind control devices we sprinkle from the clouds in order to steal all the water and master cuts of Neil Young's greatest hits (I was told this by a man wearing a full hazmat outfit at the grocery store).

As Lady Godiva disappeared, I remarked to Jody, "I can't imagine pressing my labia directly onto saltwater drenched horsehair, full gallop or not."

"You know you don't have labia, right?" Jody replied.

"True that. I'm far from an expert."

PART II

THE THROWBACK STORIES

9

THE RACCOON REMOVAL SCAM: 1983, AGE 9

My twin brother Brian and I had typical nine-year-old jobs, but lemonade stands and car washes were not bringing in the dough needed for our three-pack-a-day ammo habit. For your typical nine-year-old, these professions weren't considered age-appropriate, but if you read my first book, you know age-appropriate quit being age-appropriate soon after we figured out how to build a homemade bomb using only sparklers and tennis balls.

"We gotta go to a buck a glass," I said, frustrated with our slumping revenues.

"Nobody's gonna pay that," Brian answered, stating the obvious. Keep in mind this was 1983, before people paid more for a cup of coffee than their kid's education.

"$6.20. This ten-cents crap just ain't cuttin' it," I replied after counting up the day's bounty.

Frustrated, we chugged the Country Time goodness and headed inside. Obviously, for 10¢ a glass we were not squeezing organic lemons and agave.

A week later, my parents were having the Browns over for a barbecue. The Browns were upstanding members of the community and, depending on whom you asked, tended to dress better or tackier than our family. Mr. Brown was a nice man who had grown up in Atlanta, and therefore possessed little to no country-strength cred. He was thin with a potbelly that jutted from his frame as if he were perpetually in the act of shoplifting. The caloric fanny pack in combination with his ridiculous comb-over were killing his chances of being Matthew McConnaughey's stunt double. Mrs. Brown had one of those permanent, overly exaggerated smiles, the sure sign of an addiction to prescription meds and an upcoming nervous breakdown. My mom would joke about Mrs. Brown's 'Helmet', the infamous hairdo that went unchanged for decades. The Helmet never seemed to grow or change colors, and even the harshest weather was no match for this rock-hard sculpture. She always took quick shallow breaths; maybe fearful she would appear fat if she ever fully inflated her lungs. This woman was wound tight, and I find myself wondering if she ever stabbed anyone.

With such rock-star parents, the kids' bios are almost too predictable to type. After finally leaving the fortress of suck for college, their son ended up in rehab after driving a Pontiac Grand Am through a Hardees, the youngest daughter married a biker and now sports a matching full back and neck tattoo, and the oldest (who had the bod for it) ended up on *Girls Gone Wild*.

Sipping his sweet tea, the nectar of the gods that would later give him diabetes and lead to the removal of three of his toes, Mr. Brown waxed on about the killer raccoon harassing his cat and endangering his precious, perfectly combed kids. Even my dad, who is overly polite, was having a hard time keeping a straight face. Brian rolled his eyes. We had heard about killer raccoons and coyotes our entire childhood, as middle-aged pencil-pushing men desperately tried to concoct a life or death situation to validate their manhood and arsenal of weapons. Yes, I know raccoons carry rabies; but unless you have one caught in a leg-hold trap while trying to stuff him in a burlap sack, you'd have a hard time actually getting bit by one. Brian almost lost a thumb in the aforementioned scenario—not pretty. (My ecologically sensitive wife has yet to find out about my leg-hold trap days. Let's keep it that way please.)

"These boys could help; they catch raccoons all the time," my dad answered, trying to console the Cowardly Lion.

"Really?" Mr. Brown excitedly looked to Brian.

"Sure," Brian shrugged, not wanting to cancel our fishing trip to go help this family of five Berts (no Ernies).

"That'd be great! There's twenty bucks in it for ya. Wanna come over in the morning?"

Nothing like a little juice to get our attention. Keep in mind, this was 1983 and we were nine: this was solid money.

"We'll see you at seven," Brian answered with zero hesitation. We were early risers, and our delinquent Day-Timers were quite full. Of the two of us, Brian was always the one leaning forward on his toes, like a boxer, perpetually ready for battle or a heist. Take Robert Deniro in *GoodFellas* and dress him in cutoffs as a nine-year-old boy, and you have Brian Weathington. I was always toward the back, the *de facto* voice of reason, and the main person in charge of keeping us out of prison.

Raccoons are amazing animals: smart, opposable thumbs, can climb like squirrels, swim like otters, and do all this while wearing a pimp-ass fur coat. They are highly adaptable animals, but due to their lack of saliva glands, they need a fresh water source and usually live close to rivers and creeks. In urban settings, raccoons are unable to find their usual diet of crawfish, minnows, and frogs, and instead are forced to stalk their favorite urban prey: cat food. Raccoons love cat food and with the adjacent finger bowl it's the Waffle House of the masked bandit world. Ironically, raccoons and Waffle House waitresses have similar dental plans and breath.

Trapping a wild raccoon can be quite difficult, but an urban raccoon would be like trying to find a confederate flag at a NASCAR event. We showed up with a two-door no. 4 cage trap and a can of sardines, the one thing they love better than cat food.

We said our pleasantries and went to business; total turnaround time to set the trap was less than five minutes. Early the next morning, as the French toast hit the table, the phone rang. My dad answered.

"That's great!" he said, trying to match Mr. Brown's excitement.

When he hung up, he picked up a slice of bacon and lowered

the enthusiasm in his voice back to the appropriate level for the situation.

"You boys caught Mr. Brown's raccoon," our dad said over his cup of coffee. "Maybe you should go get it. I think he's about to wet himself."

"He's not really going to pay you to catch that raccoon?" my mom asked, grinning.

"It looks that way," I answered with a laugh.

It was not even eight in the morning and the air was starting to thicken up with Georgia summer heat. We jumped on our Spiderman bikes, both outfitted with homemade crates to carry traps, fishing rods, stringers of fish, dead squirrels, or shotguns.

Mr. Brown met us halfway up the driveway, already sporting his khaki pants and white button-down uniform. A tie was always added for church. No one in town had ever seen him dressed in anything else. I always wondered if he slept in them; having sex with a man in khaki pajamas is not exactly Fabio in a pirate outfit. We held our laughter as he flapped his arms in a crackhead version of a Grateful Dead noodle dance. He was damn excited we had saved his family from certain doom.

"You boys did it! You did it! Amazing!"

This guy was easily impressed; wait until we showed him our homemade landmines.

"I can't thank you enough," Mr. Brown said, as he handed me the twenty while Brian loaded up one angry fur ball to the back of his bike. As a tip, he also threw in a six-pack of cold Cokes in the bottles. Nice touch.

"I can't believe he really paid us," I commented, as I sipped my Coke while pedaling home.

"Beats the hell out of lemonade," Brian replied, laughing. "We need more Mr. Browns."

He rubbed his chin thoughtfully, riding with no hands, a pretty impressive move with a fifteen-pound maniac going side to side on his tailgate.

"What about the Ogdens?" I answered. The Ogdens also wore obnoxious amounts of khaki and gold-buttoned navy blazers—even the five-year-old, but he didn't know any better. They lived five miles away from Mr. Brown in a similar very exclusive neighborhood (i.e. you could only fly the Stars and Bars in the backyard). It was just far enough away that our new furry friend would not be able to find his way back to Mr. Brown's; we did have a reputation to uphold after all.

After two or three drive-bys we decided the coast was clear. The carport was around the side.

Brian took Jabba-the-Coon and introduced him to the Ogdens' cat food. Ordinarily a trapped raccoon was too busy trying to chew your face off to eat. But Jabba took the bait.

"That should do," Brian said, opening the trap. At first, Jabba acted as if he were about to set up camp on the foosball table when Brian shooed him away to the nearby woods.

"That's one lazy ass raccoon," I commented, as I loaded the cage on my bike.

A few weeks went by and we had forgotten about our obese friend.

"Nathan, Brian, telephone!" my mom yelled from the kitchen.

"I'll get it," I answered, as I ran downstairs.

"Mr. Brown tells me you boys can catch raccoons," I heard on the other end of the line.

Yahtzee!

Jabba had put on at least two or three more pounds of cat food to his thighs. He filled the trap, and was lethargically calm.

"That's a huge raccoon. Thank God he didn't kill my fluffy," Mr. Ogden said, out of breath, as he wiped his sweaty forehead with a paper towel.

I agreed, knowing Jabba couldn't have caught a rock, much less a cat.

"Mr. Brown was right; you boys know your stuff," he said as he handed us a twenty and six no name colas. They had obviously discussed our fee structure.

"How about the Suttons?" I said, back on my bike drinking the disgusting budget cola with Jabba taking a nap on the back.

"Why not?"

We biked another five miles to the next target.

Later that night in bed, while we debriefed our raccoon scam, Brian added some sprinkles.

"We need more raccoons."

"Let's put the full line out tomorrow," I answered from the top bunk.

On Saturday morning we used some bungee cords to pile three traps, a bag of cat food, and a pile of sardine cans on each bike. On Sunday morning we had two masked volunteers for the mission, one large female and one sickly looking young male. We released the female and kept the easily distinguishable runt. With a pardon from church, we biked like hell back to

Mr. Brown's house at 10:10 am in the middle of Sunday School. He never skipped—solid Christian role model.

The runt was not interested in the cat food in the carport, so we placed a large pile of cat food at the edge of the Browns' yard, hoping to lure the wild raccoon back to the house.

In the end, we had three raccoons in circulation, with six homes in the mix. Not all of them took, but in four weeks we brought in $220, seven six-packs of high-fructose corn syrup, a box of red wigglers, one jumbo bag of Charles Chips, a bundle of bottle rockets, and four 12-gauge 8 shot shotgun shells. Maybe we weren't making Christmas tree money yet, but it sure beat the hell out of selling lemonade.

No animals were injured during the telling of this story.

10

THE SECOND SLING SHOT INCIDENT: COLLEGE

Originally, there were two slingshot incidents in my first book, but as my editor rightfully pointed out, maybe one slingshot incident would suffice in the first book by an unknown author.

No one on this planet holds a grudge longer than Ray "Corndog" Womack. Be forewarned: if you have ever wronged Ray, even if it was twenty-five years ago, you will get yours—if you have not already. My only advice to you if you have ever offended Ray Womack is to track him down, drop off a new table saw, a nice bottle of bourbon, and some Byron's BBQ sandwiches, and hope it covers your debt to him.

Ray Womack was the first kid we ever met who out-badassed the Weathington Boys. When we met Ray in the third grade he already carried a knife and could drive a stick better than most amateur racecar drivers. On one of our first "play dates"

Ray hotwired the neighbor's baby blue Chevette—the getaway car, obviously—and drove us to the local pool hall where we picked the locks on the tables and used all the quarters to gamble on a punch board bingo game. My wife continues to call bullshit on this Ray driving factoid, but no one from Bremen, Georgia, does.

A few teachers made Ray's Revenge List. Brian and I once watched Ray unexpectedly smack a social studies teacher ten years after he paddled Ray for having to go to the bathroom in the seventh grade. Come to think of it, Teacher did have it coming; this was 1987—Ray was not exactly Kunta Kinte. The weird thing was that the teacher, who was actually just a coach and not really a teacher at all, never uttered a word. He knew exactly what the decade old slap upside the head was for. It was a good strategy, probably saving him from a much more severe Ray Womack beat down.

Mr. B made the mistake of failing Ray in ninth grade biology, a lapse of judgment that almost got him decapitated. Although brilliant, Ray was a crappy student in high school; he took off every religious holiday, all Mondays and every other Friday. He also worked tirelessly helping his dad in the shop to help feed the family, leaving him little energy for academics. And being from the wrong side of the tracks, not many people seemed to notice or care. But in this case, Ray was very close to passing. He was given the opportunity to earn enough extra credit to pass by being Mr. B's slave for a week. Ray was cleaning windows, organizing desks, and scraping paint off walls. Ray did the hard time, which was not the problem. The problem came when the report cards arrived and Mr. B had still failed him. Ray had been swindled.

Five years later, we were in our second year of college and home during a semester break. My parents loved for us to come home, not only because we were their sons, but also because we entertained the hell out of them. Mom routinely ditched her friends to hang out with us; bridge just didn't do it for her.

While driving by our old high school, Ray looked out the window.

"There's Mr. B cutting grass on the football field."

Mr. B had retired from teaching and now worked at the school as a maintenance man.

"Isn't that what he gets paid to do?" Brian sarcastically asked.

"I owe that bastard," Ray growled.

Brian and I had seen this side of Ray before and knew we couldn't stop it (not that we wanted to); we could only do our best to make sure Ray didn't end up in jail or kill anyone.

Brian parked the truck on a back road and we walked through the woods with Ray in front. Ray grabbed a slingshot from the bed of the truck and made us both fill our pockets with rock-hard crabapples from a tree near the school. Who needs reality television when you have a crazed country boy with a slingshot out to settle the score for a long-forgotten grievance?

Ray led us to a nice vantage point in the bleachers—as fate would have it, the same one we'd used three years earlier when we assaulted the principal's wife with two dozen eggs. We dumped the apples in a pile. Mr. B was cutting the field in concentric circles, and our base was around the thirty-yard line, making it so he would pass us at close range once on each revolution. This was going to be entertaining.

Crabapples do not fly like the ball bearings we used to thwart the TPers at our house; they have a little slice to them. Each time Mr. B passed on the tractor Ray would fire two shots off, one when he was broadside and one once his back was turned. The apples were flying by his head so fast he thought they were bees and began swatting at them. With each pass, Ray got more frustrated as each apple would spin off its path, narrowly missing his noggin and denying Ray his vengeance.

He was almost done cutting the field and we were getting low on apples. Ray had two passes left and eight apples. He was getting pissed and decided that he would risk getting busted and launch during his approach as well.

Mr. B swatted at the two "bees" as they flew straight by his face at breakneck speed. As he came broadside, I could see sweat dripping from Ray's nose as he propped the upper half of his body on the bleacher to steady himself. Just as Luke Skywalker abandoned his targeting computer in the final seconds of his successful attack on the Death Star, Ray relaxed and let go of his careful aiming. He pulled back hard, yet relaxed, and let that crabapple go where God intended.

This apple, for whatever reason, did not swerve; it flew true, and that is all Ray needed. The apple hit the poor man right in the ear. I could not watch; I knew he was going to fall off the tractor and get chopped up by the giant Bush Hog he was towing. He did fall off the tractor, but luckily the impact of the apple smacked him so hard he flew clear of the blade.

Had Ray not put the extra pull on this specific shot, he might have dissected him like a frog in a blender.

Ray stared, extremely pleased. Vengeance was his, no matter how ridiculous. Brian laughed himself to tears. I seemed to be the only one who breathed a sigh of relief when Mr. B finally sat up and showed signs of life. He was a tough old bird. He got up, looked around for what he must have thought was the nastiest hornet on the planet, and chased after his tractor now idling against the fence.

Payback can be a bitch, and sometimes it's just a crabapple upside your damn face.

11

POACHING

Doves love to eat watermelon seeds. Sadly, they rarely get to eat their favorite food, for two reasons. First, watermelons tend to be harvested by their rightful owners. And second, it's difficult for a four-and-a-half ounce bird to fly in a straight line while carrying the requisite Swiss Army Knife needed to cut into this summer delicacy. This might seem like the most random-ass piece of nature trivia you've heard in a while, but this little factoid entertained me every summer from 1987 to 1992.

If you grew up in The South, most likely you already know that people shoot doves for sport. In case no one in your family owns camouflage, I should point out that these are the same cute little birds you see released at weddings. There are two things you should know about dove hunting. First, they are damn tasty, especially when wrapped in bacon. (But then again,

I believe a man would eat his own pinkie toe if it was served to him wrapped in bacon with a colorful toothpick stuck in it.) Second, they are damn hard to shoot; they can reach speeds of up to 55 mph (that's 88 km/h for you metrically leaning socialists).

It was mid-summer, and the Georgia heat was sweltering around triple digits. It was a good day for poaching. It was 1989, and Brian, Ray, and I were driving down some dirt roads in a rural part of Georgia that even country people avoid. Imagine the Jeff Foxworthy setup of "You might be a redneck if …" with the punch-line delivered by Cormac McCarthy—yeah, that dark and that funny. If you have ever spent much time in such a place, or have ever ridden a Greyhound bus for more than a few minutes, you tend to show little surprise when police uncover a serial killer, meth lab, or rattlesnake Christianity.

"I think the melons are ready," Ray said, one hand on the wheel, with a Yoo-hoo in the other. The Yoo-hoo was washing down our large bag of boiled peanuts we had lifted from People Pleaser, a local convenience store. We still had one more year until we could legally drive, but we had all been driving for a few years at this point (or a decade in Ray's case).

"They look it. And I see some of our friends in the tree," I answered loudly, pointing at close to thirty doves perched toward the top.

You had to scream in Ray's Dodge truck to be heard. It was missing the front windshield, cab, hood, all the quarter panels, the bed, grill, muffler, lights, and dash. Simply put, it was a seat, frame, and 357 V6 engine.

You know, this requires a bit of explanation. Allow me to digress.

***

The Dodge was a white and rust-colored 1980 Ram D150 ½-ton long-bed pick up. A year earlier, Ray discovered The Dodge with a $500 OBO plywood sign parked in a rougher part of town (or lack of town, more precisely).

"Pull over," Ray asked me. He proceeded up to the door of a house that looked destined to be part of a twister-aftermath story on Channel Five ("It sounded like a train!"). The optimistic seller of the truck was buckling one strap on his shirtless overalls and kicking a fighting rooster out from under his feet as they returned to the truck.

"I'm 'fraid it don't run. You'll need tow it," the owner said in a southern drawl that was so thick it was barely decipherable. He then spit with accuracy, in that way only dippers and chewers can.

"Yeah, that's what I figgar," Ray said, as he tinkered under the hood while Brian and I stood there, confused as to why Ray would want a truck that didn't run. Without shutting the hood, he stepped back, reaching for his wallet.

"I can give ya two," he said, offering more than I thought it was worth.

"Four," the owner countered.

"All I got's two."

"Three."

"Two, and I'll have it out of here in thirty minutes."

"Deal," the owner said after a few seconds of contemplation. He then shook hands with Ray, obviously thinking about how happy his wife would be when she returned to a truckless front yard.

Ray actually only had $100; Brian and I threw in another $80 plus two boxes of 20 gauge shells for 50-percent ownership of this worthless heap. After Ray handed the man the money and ammo he went back under the hood with a flathead screwdriver and a large Estwing framing hammer. The owner was quite proud of himself, selling this worthless truck to a fifteen-year-old boy who was naïve enough to think he could actually make it run. Ray then hauled back and, with one loud thud, smacked the crap out of something under the hood. He then stepped down and got into the driver's seat. He shifted the manual transmission into neutral, pumped the gas pedal three or four times, and turned the key. It turned over; the battery still had some life in it.

"Yer gonna have to tow it thar, boy," the owner said.

His mouth continued to mouth out numbers as he did some long division in his head, trying to figure out how many PBRs he could get for $180. This was a couple of decades before hipsters decided this budget beer was cool, and subsequently drove the price up. What a bunch of idiots.

Ray didn't acknowledge the man. He was the Truck Whisperer and in full concentration—listening, feeling, watching, and smelling everything the truck wanted to tell him. When I saw Ray's blank stare, I started to figure it out.

Vrooooom, gug, gug, gug, Vrooooom, gug, gug, gug …

The truck came to life as we all stepped back from the dust and fumes. Brian, covering his face, slammed the hood, and Ray was already slamming it into gear. Fearing it would stall, and not wanting to let up on the gas, nor wanting to have to renegotiate, Ray peeled out of the man's yard leaving two nice tire tracks next to his mailbox. It was unavoidable. Brian and I were laughing our asses off as Ray rocketed down the road in a cloud of smoke. The back right tire was flat as a pancake and made a rhythmic thumping noise as he drove over the hill with Free Bird blaring over the speakers.

"Hey, hey, hey!" the owner yelled, walking after the truck.

He was second-guessing his ace negotiating skills at this point.

"That lil' shit even got my Skynyrd tape," he said under his breath, turning to look at Brian and me.

"Well, ain't that somethin'," I said with a shrug, already getting into the truck with Brian. Neither of us wanted to hang around this neck of the woods any longer than we had to. The man said nothing; he got swindled by a fifteen-year-old, but a deal was a deal, and he knew that. Now three fifteen-year-old boys owned a $180 truck; it was *Mad Max* meets *The Dukes of Hazzard*, and we would be lucky to make it out alive.

***

Back to the watermelons.

"How many shells you got?" Ray asked.

Brian reached under the seat of The Dodge and pulled out two boxes of 12-gauge shells.

"We're almost full," Brian answered, shaking the two boxes. Everyone knew he meant fifty rounds; we knew our 25 times-tables better than most.

"I might have a box at the house," Ray replied.

"I'll get a knife," I added.

From Ray's house, we hiked through the woods a mile or two back to the field. We got a few birds out of the tree before we had even started.

"I need to warm up," Brian said with a smile.

"Same," I replied as I gathered some large sticks. I proceeded to ram five sticks at varying heights into the soft ploughed field. I then stuck a watermelon on top of each stick. The Watermelon family consisted of a dad, mom, and three kids. We took our spots about ten feet away.

"Eyes closed? Ready? Go!" Brian instructed. We all three unloaded on the Melon family. They really had no chance. Gallagher's Sledge-O-Matic was a Q-tip compared to the firepower we were packing. Not only did this help us get ready, it also spread the delicious watermelon seeds out for our prey. We strolled toward the middle of the field, busting open a few more melons for the birds to eat. This was a year or two before it occurred to us that fencing the melons could be a lucrative career. Once we reached our blind, we needed our own snack. We each used the knife to carve out the hearts of three or four near-boiling watermelons for lunch while we waited for the flock to return. The rest of the day consisted of eating watermelons with the occasional break to slaughter a slew of Noah's favorite bird. With a pile of birds each, we were about to head home.

"What's that noise?" Brian asked, stepping out of the blind for a better look. He spotted a mean-looking mouth-breather, still a ways down the hill but huffing at a good pace. "Farmer! Giddy up!"

We were on our feet and moving toward our getaway trail. This was far from the first time we had been required to run for our lives. We had a decent head start, so we weren't nervous at first.

"They got a gun," Brian yelled between breaths. Everyone quickly found that next gear, which isn't easy carrying a 12-gauge and a pillowcase full of birds.

"You alright?" I yelled back, noticing Ray was falling behind.

"I don't think I'm gonna make it," he answered.

"Really?" I said, surprised. We had barely run a quarter of a mile, and we were all in peak delinquent shape. But the anchor slowing him down was not cardiovascular in nature; it was more intestinal.

"I ate too many melons. I think I'm gonna shit my pants."

"What are you talking about?" Brian shouted back. "I feel fine!"

"Well, yeah, but you're no threat to shit *my* pants now, are you?"

At this, we all three began to laugh, although Ray's guffaws were somewhat subdued by his already clenched stomach muscles.

"He'll be comin' over the hill any time," I said. "What're we gonna do?"

"Hide me," Ray said, jumping into a giant pile of briars and bushes with his gun and bag of birds. Brian and I threw anything we could find on top of him: a few small pine trees, a cardboard box, and an old tire.

"You good?" I asked.

"Go!" was the reply.

Brian and I started running just as the farmer cracked the hill. He was busy trying to get his sights on us and drove right past Ray hidden in his brambled latrine. Brian and I made the escape route and were back to Ray's house in fifteen minutes. An hour later, Ray came shuffling into the yard, missing not one but both socks.

"You okay there, slim?" Brian asked a pale-faced Ray.

"Yeah, but I don't think I'll be eating hot melons any time soon."

With color back in his face, Ray pulled his fifth dove from the campfire. As fifteen-year-old boys tend to do for no apparent reason, we stayed up the rest of the night to keep the fire going before embarking on another senseless adventure the next day.

Looking back, my childhood could be represented by a cross between a Norman Rockwell painting and an NRA poster.

PART III

RETURN TO THE MOTHERLAND

12

THE MEAT ROCKET INCIDENT OF 1999

I know it's hard to believe, but there aren't many gay bars in Bremen, Georgia, population 3,500. There are no bars for that matter—might lead to dancing—and Kevin Bacon can't live everywhere at once. But where Georgia might fall short, our southern neighbor dispenses sinful liquids every fifty feet or so. It's hard for me to even think about the Florida years without ending up in an emotional fetal position. My insecurities and corresponding debauchery reached an all-time high while I lived in Florida. My booze-soaked personality at the time was barely tolerable.

I was on the verge of having to go to several types of support meetings; alcoholism is the easiest to understand. When you're drinking light beer with your buddies, but you chase each pitcher with a dirty martini made from rotgut gin, and you're still called on to drive everyone home, it's time to tone it back.

I was game for anything, and nothing was too crazy, warped, or idiotic.

At the time, I was still working as a civil engineer. When I wasn't waking up on a beach unsure if I was staring at the Atlantic or the Gulf, my day job was designing parking lots for Kroger. Thank goodness I had taken differential equations in college, as I was now tasked with drawing parallel lines.

My best friend Tony desperately wanted to out-crazy me. He figured with my sheltered childhood in rural Georgia, I wasn't ready to play with the big boys down in big-city Florida. Tony was, and maybe still is, Mr. Gay Florida. He wrongly assumed this gave him the upper hand. This man was smoking hot, charming, rich, funny, and talented. All gay men wanted him, and straight women desperately wanted to convert him. He reminded me of a thin George Clooney—in assless chaps. But unlike the caricature gay stereotype, I wouldn't have described Tony as effeminate; quite the opposite, actually. He looked and carried himself more like a Marlboro man than a backup dancer for L.L. Cool J. Everyone was drawn to him as if he were a spiritual leader (a spiritual leader who enjoyed snorting the occasional body shot off the bartender's six pack). As a spiritual leader, Tony would be a cross between Jim Bakker and a young, charismatic Johnny Depp.

Like me, Tony had left his small rural hometown the day after high school graduation. I wasn't sure what I was looking for, but Tony knew exactly what he was looking for. Once Tony found a place where he could drive a Mazda Miata and roller blade in day glow short shorts without ridicule, he set up shop and quickly became the hottest thing on eight wheels.

A bet had to be laid. It was a large bet, the details of which I'm still uncomfortable sharing with the general public. Let's just say it was a LARGE bet, and for the sake of this story, visualize a briefcase full of cash or anything that would motivate you to risk compromising your career, pride, and soul, which is what I did to help myself sleep for a few months after the incident.

"If I shock you, make you uncomfortable, or out-party you, I win," Tony said to solidify the terms of the bet. We now lounged on the sidewalk in front of the second bar we'd been kicked out of that night.

"Dream on," I answered, not even listening, just instinctively talking shit.

"So?" Tony asked, extending his hand.

"Whatever, I'm in," I slurred, as we affirmed a bet that would almost kill both of us over the next six months.

This bet would take me to places I wish I didn't know existed. Today, I try to convince myself these places are rural legends, only to wake in cold sweats remembering that not only was I there, I also happened to be the star attraction at the Meat Rocket on that flaccid Tuesday afternoon. It was all a ridiculous blur of sin: topless billiards, streaking, pregnant strippers and hookers, and sexcapades most men think only happen on the Internet. Sundays we could be found grasping for a quart of rubbing alcohol to soak our loofas in.

For the record, neither Tony nor I masterminded the pregnant strippers/hookers situation. It was three in the morning and someone else was driving. The driver, whom we'd just met that night, decided it would be a good idea to pull up to one of the many neon "Lingerie Model" signs you see all too frequently along Florida highways. I later found out we were in the same building where Peewee Herman got busted; in other words, a place steeped in quality, relevant American history. The parking lot was empty, and the sound of cicadas was loud and steady. Tony and I left the hot, salty Florida air and walked into the cool, brightly lit, oxygen-depleted waiting room of this house of fashion. The surreal décor, which included a velvet painting of a panther next to a poster of Grave Digger (the monster truck, not the wrestler), combined with the chill, slapped us into sobriety. Tony casually picked up a *Florida Sportsman* magazine. The owner of the establishment strolled out with her pregnant belly leading the way and, with a wink, led our driver by the hand back to her cave. This was not our tour guide's first rodeo. Our driver was your generic Florida male: fish-embossed shirt, visor, goatee, short hair, raccoon style tan lines around his eyes, mildly to extremely racist depending on how much he drank, loved a good fist fight, and bragged about going to the University of Florida as if that was something you should admit.

"This is just depressing," Tony said, looking up from his article on Redfish.

"I agree. Let's get out of here."

Tony grabbed the keys from the coffee table. This was the last time we saw our driver. We didn't need to be associating with people with lower morals than our own, plus Tony and I didn't like splitting our handle of gin three ways.

We bought our booze in bulk and stuck to the basics: gin, vodka, and whiskey. We skipped the hard stuff and only drank beer on the days we'd be flying small aircraft. It only took six Coors Light before Tony started to proposition me. He was sure a little male sexual aggression would freak me out. This only made me laugh, and given my insecurities at the time, I liked the attention. It's also tough to startle someone who has lost all feeling in his extremities.

Before our lives were really going off the rails, I briefly had a girlfriend. Tony had actually set us up; they were best friends. I would bring up the fact that her best friend was trying to have sex with me, and she would just laugh. Tony was so charming, or gay, or both, that he could try to have sex with his best friend's boyfriend and she wouldn't even get mad. He should have run for president.

"Ready for *my* bar there, Bumpkin?" Tony asked me around 11:00 pm. Bumpkin was his pet name for me. We were at the third stop on our tour of places that serve vodka in pint glasses, and were starting to smell of low-tide dipped in ass.

"Bring it, bitch," I shouted at the same moment someone inevitably unplugged the jukebox. I felt like a drunken Bruce Leroy in *The Last Dragon.*

Tony drove us (I do not condone this behavior) a few miles away to the nice part of town. The valet parked our car as we sauntered up the large flight of granite stairs. All modesty aside, Tony and I did make a nice couple. We were tall, tan, and tight, and collectively we could really turn some heads. As I entered the room, the smell of freshly shucked oysters and sophistication hit me. This place was impressive: silvered mirrors, antique couches, fifty kinds of tequila, chandeliers, cigars, ten-foot solid wood doors, and not a drop of light beer or alcoholic Slush Puppie. Everyone in the joint was dressed to the nines; nobody was working the official uniform of the white Florida male. My see-through skin-tight silk shirt now seemed more logical. No one wore socks, and everyone had shaved within the last few minutes. Although I did think myself hot-shit at the time, I was looking pretty homely compared to this group of men, who all could have passed as David Beckham's stunt double. A cannibal would have starved in this joint; I didn't see anyone with over 5-percent body fat. Everyone was smiling and laughing; I only hoped I was in on the joke.

"Are you sure you can handle this?" Tony asked hopefully.

"What do you mean? This place rocks."

"Tony, can I buy your friend here a drink?" a stocky dude said, sidling up.

I'd never had anyone buy me a drink, let alone a stranger. I was flattered and giddy; it was like a first date. This steed cut in on Tony like he was a yard sale.

"Sure," Tony and I said, simultaneously. Tony sauntered off, leaving me alone with my new best friend, figuring this was the perfect way to finally make me uncomfortable. I barely even noticed. But Tony could have at least given a courtesy pause, or maybe even pretended he was going to fight for my honor. What a shitty boyfriend.

"What are you drinking there?" I asked New Best Friend, who was holding what looked like a goldfish bowl.

"Bombay Sapphire martini."

"You mean a cosmopolitan, right?" I yelled over Prince's *Raspberry Beret* in the background, inadvertently stereotyping my new best friend.

"Nope," New Best Friend replied coldly, slightly annoyed at my mild homophobic slur. "You know, cold gin, a little vermouth. Wake up in a stranger's house. Martini."

"I'll have what he's having," I said with enthusiasm to our server, a dead ringer for a young Daniel Day Lewis. I was finally amongst my people, men who drank like men, no more of this Bud Light Lime bullshit.

We drank toe-to-toe for the rest of the night, and having started drinking at eleven in the morning, I was not fairing very well. Today, I can barely drink three beers without puking. Oh, how the pendulum swings. When I started singing Madonna's *Holiday* at the top of my lungs with the crowd, Tony knew he would need to take this party to the next level if he wanted to win the bet.

"So … we'll see you *there*," New Best Friend said to Tony.

"We're on our way," Tony excitedly answered, as if he had just discovered the flux capacitor.

Back in the parking lot, I asked Tony where *there* was.

"You'll see," he answered, Jack Palance style, stumbling into the driver's seat.

I never get car sick and, at that time, never puked when I was drinking. However, the combo of riding in a car drunk really pushed me over the edge. My head was out the window, begging the wind to suck the toxins from my body as bugs hit my unflinching face and teeth every few seconds. The hot damp air of the swamp felt nice.

Hang on.

"Why the hell're we in a swamp?"

"We're almost *there*," he glittered.

Every time I looked over, Tony gave me an odd wink with a raised eyebrow, like a flirtatious Dwayne "The Rock" Johnson. My head had stopped spinning, but my stomach now felt like a gin-filled piñata. Tony turned off our radio, and I could feel my face turning pale as I heard a faint Beastie Boys bass-line coming from the cypress trees. Could Tony see my eye twitch?

"Where's that music coming from?" I asked.

Tony only responded with a maniacal laugh that went on too long.

Tony was not going to strangle me and dump my body in the swamp, so why had I stopped breathing? Was it the gayness? Besides the cosmopolitan crack, I now thought of myself as quite worldly. There was no way I was homophobic: my best friend was gay, after all.

Like other kids growing up in small towns, especially in the buckle of the Bible Belt, I did inherit a certain amount of lowbrow, uneducated vocabulary around people's sexuality, but that had faded years before this incident. Maybe deep down, under the layers of booze, under my self-proclaimed worldliness, somehow against my will, hate-filled church sermons and good-ole-boy epithets from my childhood were woven deep into my intoxicated brain. Or maybe straight men are just naturally, on some level, uncomfortable around extreme gayness? Who knows, but Tony knew it was there, and his plan all along was to dig deep enough to find it.

Soon we arrived at the bumpiest cinder block shack on the planet.

"What's this place?" I asked, wiping the cold, wind-swept tears from my face.

"The Swamp."

"No shit."

"That's the name of the bar."

"Oh."

"Ready?"

"Let's do this!" was the last arrogant thing I said that year.

I paid my $5 cover and was given two shots of decent tequila, not a bad deal. So far, so good.

The next thing I see is what looks like an underwear model, butt ass naked, except for his Reebok Velcro high-tops and scrunchy socks. So technically, I guess he was a Reebok/scrunchy sock model. My face felt like a George Foreman Grill and cold chills went down my neck.

My first thought was, *Weird, he has no body hair or tan lines.*

Mr. Reeboks was the doorman, and we were officially not in Georgia anymore. With his back to us, his knees locked out straight; he appeared to be stretching his hairless hamstrings. I was unsure if he was preparing for an athletic event or if stretching was the event.

"Welcome to The Swamp," he said, straightening himself, as if he were merely stamping my coffee club card. At this point, I was trying my best to blend in—I didn't want Tony to know he finally had me.

"How ya doin' there, Bumpkin?" Tony asked, now in full Mayor of Gay Florida mode as he gave the nod-and-point to most of the men around the bar like a seasoned politician.

"Uhh … fine," I said, as my voice cracked like a branded donkey.

Unable to stare the doorman in the eyes, I let my eyes drift southward. Ouch! A penis the size of a can of hairspray was staring back at me, challenging me to an arm wrestling contest I would surely lose. It looked like a carnie holding an eggplant. Damn thing had an elbow. At this point, I was no longer talking or even bobbing my head to the beat, and Tony knew he had won.

Although nothing to look at on the outside, The Swamp was quite nice on the inside. A fancy three-sided wooden bar was staffed by three shirtless men (as to be expected). And these boys were slinging shots like Wet Willies on speed. The crowd was loud, and would break out in organized chants, songs, and dances, none of which I had been given the songbook to.

After the performance by the 6'6" lady, who swung from and broke one of the water pipes on stage, my vision started closing in. Trying to sober up, I left the stage show and grabbed a pitcher of water. Splashing my face, I rounded the corner and ran face first into my boss at the engineering firm, who I was pretty sure was in the closet. (A little context: the owner of the firm was known to fire someone for being a Democrat, so I'm not condemning my boss for keeping his personal life separate from work. Tony and I both knew the owner of the firm was keeping his fetish for Vaseline and spatulas a secret, so what's the difference?)

"Hey, Ted," I yelled with water streaming down my face, not able to summon the energy to say much more.

"Uh … hey, Nathan," my boss answered shyly, followed by what seemed like five minutes of uncomfortable silence.

"I'm not gay," we both said, my voice a millisecond behind his, as if we were making an international call.

"No, no, I'm really not gay," I told my boss.

"No, no, I'm really not gay," he answered.

"Seriously, I'm not," looking for an out.

"Me either," Ted replied.

Cue painful silence. I can assure you two men yelling I'M NOT GAY in the gayest bar on Earth is about as awkward as it sounds. After a deep search for my two remaining brain cells, I leaned in.

"I'll never mention tonight to another living person, including you," I whispered in his ear.

His face relaxed. We had a moment. It was a moment between men, like the trenches of war, team sports, or a musical rendition of *Rocky III*. He gave me a nod; nothing else needed to be said. We both kept our pact, until recently, when I decided to start selling jokes for a living. But I've hidden enough details to cover the trail.

I stumbled outside, too gun shy to use the bathroom.

4:00 am: It was over; I curled up on the hood of Tony's car, ready for the shit-show to end.

"You gonna make it?" Tony asked as he slid me off his hood

and into the passenger seat.

"Ummph," is all I could get out with my Adam's apple propped on the glass in my window.

"You know you lost the bet, so don't bother lying."

"Ummph."

Thankfully, I woke up alone in my own bed, unsure how I got there. Although disgustingly dirty, my clothes were still on, and at first glance I did not see any tattoos or piercings—all good things. After eight waffles and three pots of coffee, I started to piece the night together. A small pink sticky note was on the door. After I rubbed the doughnut glaze from my eyes, I could decipher the hieroglyphics.

Better start waxing, Bumpkin.

13

EBONY AND IVORY

Savannah is what is right about The South; it has ambience to its core: the restaurants and bars transport you to another time, and you will inevitably end up in bed with whomever you take to dinner, so please choose your date wisely and do not order the roast beef or raw oysters.

I know, I know, we've all heard the nonsense about oysters being an aphrodisiac, but spare me. They will, in fact, give you severe runs if you eat too many. As a man who once split a bushel of oysters and a case of Corona with a woman just outside the Flora-Bama, I consider myself somewhat of an authority on the subject. Heed my warning.

Our plane touched down in Savannah and, having not lived in The South for fifteen years, I began spontaneously sweating the second we left the air-conditioned terminal. I'd flown in with two of my rougher friends. They also began perspiring, and the smell of Jim Beam filled the taxi. Although I outweighed them by a hundred pounds, these boys drink more before lunch than I can in a month. For me to survive this weekend, I would need to hide the fact I usually go to bed by nine, and that the most exciting party I'd been to in the last five years involved a game of pin the tail on the salmon (our family is really into fishing). My wife was unable to make the wedding, which was probably for the best, as we all have a few friends we don't want, or need, our wife to meet.

We were in town for my best friend Doug's wedding. Doug is from Eclectic, Alabama. I challenge you to find a more ironically named town anywhere in the world. It has 656 residents, all of whom have one of three last names (or more in the case of hyphenated names). There is one broken caution light in the middle of town and, not including Doug's uncle's Peach Wine (aka tinted moonshine), there is not a drip of hooch for sale. The fact the medical clinic is in the same room as the video store is the clincher. "Well, Jimmy, it appears you caught syphilis from your cousin Britney-Nicole, but be sure to check out *Rambo 6*. Stallone really kicks some ass in this one." There are three races in Eclectic: white, red, and really red. Doug's family was from the highbrow white side of town (i.e. they had running water).

The bride was awkwardly out of Doug's league both in looks and intellect. This isn't part of some rehearsal dinner toast to kiss up to the in-laws; she was in fact a solid nine. To squeak out a five, Doug would've needed to wax his entire body, win the lottery, fast for six months, and ride up on a white stallion. Brother must have had game though. The bride was from

Atlanta, and her family was the exact opposite color of my buddy's cracker ass, and normally would never associate with his kind, nor should they.

The one potential hiccup was that Doug had to meet and win over his future wife's eight older brothers three weeks before the wedding. Yes, eight. No one bought their tickets until after we had confirmation that Doug had survived. Daryl, the oldest of the eight very muscular, very scary brothers called and invited Doug to join them in his man cave.

Doug was your typical scared-shitless, skinny Caucasian boy. But after two weeks of sweating, he finally sauntered up and knocked on the basement door, prepared to ask eight very large black men if they would be okay with a small white man marrying their smart, younger beautiful sister. What could possibly go wrong?

Doug's hands shook as he knocked on the door. Daryl greeted him at the door and led him into a dark smoky room with a pool table in the center. Some of the brothers nodded and continued to shoot some eight ball, while the others were finishing up a poker game.

After some brief introductions, Daryl decided it was time for a little hazing.

"Want something to drink?" Daryl asked, passing over a forty of Colt 45. Having met Daryl, an accountant, I'm pretty sure he doesn't drink Colt 45 in his normal day-to-day life, and most likely bought this specifically to screw with Doug.

"Heck, yeah, I could use a drink," Doug said, as he chugged down four fingers of the malt liquor goodness in one gulp.

Roger, one of the other brothers, gave Daryl a sideways look. Maybe they'd underestimated little Doug. It just so happens, Doug was conceived, raised, and grew up in a bar. This is not a figure of speech. Doug's parents owned and operated The Shack, a country juke joint on the outskirts of Eclectic. The Shack was down a one-lane dirt road in the middle of a grove of pine trees, and conveniently just over the county line, and therefore the only legal place to buy booze within a fifty-mile radius. Doug's family lived in an apartment in the back and he spent his childhood playing pinball, eating peanuts, and stealing shots of Blue Curacao as a toddler.

"You guys shootin' some stick?" Doug asked as he sauntered toward the pool table, picking up and testing a cue.

Br'er Rabbit had landed.

"Ten bucks a game okay with you?" Ed asked in a deep voice, also trying to throw Doug off his game with a little manly gambling.

"Works for me. How 'bout five bucks a ball?" Doug suggested, as he knocked back another few fingers of malt delight. Doug made quick work of the pool table and had a pocket full of cash before anyone knew what had happened. Doug was now onto his second forty when Daryl lit up a gorilla finger of a joint.

"You want a toke of this?" Daryl asked in a smug voice, in a last ditch effort to make Doug uncomfortable.

"You betcha," Doug said, as he sucked on the giant joint as if he were trying to turn a beach ball inside out. This was straw compared to the high quality weed Doug had imported from Canada. He could have smoked three bales of this lightweight stuff and still been able to drive a full-size U-Haul from Atlanta, Georgia, to Whitefish, Montana, in two days and eighteen hours while only listening to Neil Diamond's Greatest Hits on repeat.

Doug is not a casual weed smoker; he began smoking soon after he was bumped from the #1 to the #2 pencils at the Eclectic elementary school. Weed is more like Doug's adult blankee than the infamous gateway drug (although it is the gateway drug to carpentry, I've heard). Like any professional weed smoker, Doug held the smoke in his lungs as he reclined back on the sofa. After ten or fifteen seconds he then let the cloud of smoke escape in a giant smoke ring, knowing that he had squeezed out every morsel of THC from the medicinal herb.

By the time they got out the Hennessey, Doug was family, and singing along to NWA's *Straight Outta Compton* at the top of his lungs.

Having won over the brothers, it was now time to plan an epic interracial wedding. I begged and pleaded for the wedding to be held in Eclectic for my own personal amusement, but Doug's soon-to-be wife stepped in and pointed out the obvious. Namely, that the location of their wedding would not be chosen to help one of Doug's friends write jokes about the event. She is the brains of the operation, as I mentioned.

The wedding was perfect. The ceremony was in one of Savannah's lovely outdoor squares, with her smooth-ass preacher brother officiating. This was the opposite of most southern weddings (most southern girls spend more money and time planning their weddings than their marriages). Nobody gave a damn about what font was on the napkins. They focused on the basics:

1. Make sure you are marrying the right person.

2. Lots of booze.

3. Music that you dance to the beat of instead of the words (this might confuse some Baptists).

4. Enough food to sober up the riffraff so they don't embarrass the groom.

If you are missing one or more from this list, call the wedding off—at best, you are throwing a very boring party. If you're hoping there will be dancing at your wedding, you will need a lot of numbers two and three. You can't expect sober white people to dance to bad music. That's just absurd.

I can't even begin to count the number of southern weddings I've been to where the bride was a sobbing mess. They've just been bombarded with too much damn Disney and rom-coms. This princess bullshit we subject our young girls to is out of control, and does not go away with adulthood. I've been to multiple weddings where the girls actually wore crowns (tiaras, technically, as if that's any better). What are you the princess of—the trailer park? And how long do you keep the title—until the next girl from your neighborhood gets married? Am I supposed to bow to you now? Because I seem to remember you screwing our star halfback in the back of a pickup truck down at the gravel pit back in high school. These girls have been brainwashed to live their entire lives for this one perfect day, a day where they are the center of attention and they can pretend they're Princess Diana instead of Tracey who earns $8.25 an hour and steals condoms from Walgreens. By the way, Princess Diana got divorced and died with her sugar daddy in a car crash. Or do you want to be Rachel from *Friends* and marry Ross? That's your dream man? Really? Ross? Ross wouldn't know the difference between a lug nut and a coconut, not to mention the fact that he also has the added baggage of being fictional. And it's always a good idea to start your new life together $26,000 in debt: it gives your new marriage some unneeded stress to bond over. And if everything on this one day does not go according to the perfect script that the old anti-Semitic man who had a castle and a mouse fetish predicted, the girl's life is over and she will collapse into tears.

At Doug's wedding, once the food was gone, the music was turned up and the party filled the southern home, which smelled of two centuries worth of cornbread. When the bride's Aunt Jackie backed-that-thang-up against one of the deacons of the First (and only) Baptist Church of Eclectic, Alabama, I knew The South was taking the next logical step toward full integration.

"You know, thar just like us. They go to church, play golf, love barbecue. Thar really ain't no damn difference," the groom's Uncle Jethro (real name) told me, in what was most likely one of the greatest philosophical discoveries of his life.

So, barbecue, for my Canadian readers, is a verb in Canada and a noun in The South. You barbecue burgers, fish, or godforbid, even vegetables in Canada. You eat barbecue in Georgia. This linguistic nuance still baffles my Canadian wife. Barbecue is pork and my people may not have invented the pig, but they sure as hell perfected it. Southerners are quite fond of swine—all Southerners I might add. Which makes racial slurs involving pork very confusing.

There is the well-known racial stereotype about African Americans loving ribs, fried chicken, and watermelon, which is easily the most confusing and illogical racist slur of all time. But if Uncle Jethro can admit that we all enjoy these delicacies, can we please put this nonsensical racial stereotype to rest.

Growing up The Deep South, my brain almost over-heated on many occasions trying to solve the ribs, fried chicken, and watermelon riddle. So, let me get this straight: 'those people' really like ribs, fried chicken, and watermelon ... and that's bad? Is it bad because they eat them, or because they like them? As a ten-year-old boy growing up in The South, this riddle confused the hell out of me. I loved ribs, fried chicken, and watermelon. But of course, I didn't have the self-confidence to stand up and admit publicly my love toward this trifecta of goodness. This is where the panic set in (I was an odd kid). What if someone found out that I loved ribs, fried chicken, and watermelon? Would I be ostracized from the village? Or worse, would I lose all ribs, fried chicken, and watermelon eating privileges? All white Southerners eat, and love ribs, fried chicken, and watermelon. It would make sense to be prejudiced against people who do *not* like these three Southern Staples. You just can't trust a man who is not slightly aroused by the idea of gnawing on a full rack until it looks like a stack of white piano keys.

After the reception, and after the after-party, there were not many civilized people left: Doug, a few of his younger illiterate kinfolk, me, my buddies, and the bride were all who remained in a dark bar, well off the main drag.

In case you're not from The South, southern men have a peculiar way of talking to each other, especially when drunk. We endlessly talk shit—it's the backbone of all male-male relationships in The South. I met Doug talking shit, and it has never let up for more than five minutes over the last two decades.

I met Doug in the kitchen of the Terra Cotta restaurant in Auburn, Alabama. It was my first week at work, and I was assigned the job of chopping carrots next to Doug, whom I had just met. A few minutes later, his new young girlfriend walked up and gave Doug a nice wet kiss on the mouth.

As she exited the kitchen, I never looked up from my carrots and asked, "Does she kiss everyone here like that, or just you and me?"

Not knowing me from Adam, Doug sat his knife down and glared furiously at me with his cute little baby blue eyes. Doug now had two, and only two, options: he either had to whoop my ass, or we were going to be lifelong friends. Doug, not wanting to get his country ass kicked, chose the less violent route (see how that works). The tension seemed unbearable, as Doug continued to stare at me while I chopped carrots.

He then busted out laughing. "You're a weird dude."

"Yeah," I replied, "I get that sometimes."

Doug and I will talk shit about anything. We've argued about which of us has the nicest legs to the point where we've performed 'leg offs', where we're forced to model our bare legs for analysis in front of drunken strangers. We've arm-wrestled each other and strangers. We've competed in the usual *Raiders of the Lost Ark* drinking contest, which along with smoking weed are the only two points I will concede to Doug. We've raced down the street like escaped mental patients (I blew his doors off, by the way). Horseshoes, pool, darts, trying to pick up women, you name it, and Doug and I have talked shit about and competed at it.

"Bullshit, you had a head start. You knew I was on shrooms. That's cheating," Doug drunkenly yelled across the table.

"Bitch, ya know I'm faster than you. Look at those bird legs, there's no way they can compete with these quadzillas," I yelled back, now hiking up my pants and flexing in front of a confused and annoyed table of patrons.

"Wanna make it interesting?" Doug challenged.

"Whatever's in there," I answered, throwing my wallet on the table.

I'm no baller, but neither are any of my friends, so even a couple of hunnies is enough to add some real heat to the moment. Doug flinched, sobered up a bit, and knew (like my relationship with tequila) that this was not a dance that would end well for him. But because it was his wedding, and because I wanted to have some fun, I gave Doug an out.

"How bout this. Ya know you can't beat me, even if you ain't gonna admit it in front of your new wife. However, not only am I saying you can't out run me, but you can't out run anybody."

"Anybody? Who's anybody?"

"The first person we meet outside those doors," I answered, motioning outside.

"Bring it, muthafucka," Doug said, reaching out to shake

hands.

The rest of our party, along with a couple stragglers who were intrigued by the potential contest, all walked outside, drinks still in hand. Unbeknownst to Doug, I had already been outside and scoped some talent. Just outside the bar were two ladies that were still working, if you know what I mean.

But when it came time to approach the ladies, I froze. I merely talk a big game. Luckily, our friend RiffRaff #2 seemed unusually comfortable with the situation, and walked up to the ladies as if he were ordering a cheeseburger. He briefed the ladies on the situation and introduced them to the group.

"You ladies wanna have some fun?" I asked.

"Always, baby," the white woman with the strawberry colored wig replied.

"Well, actually, we don't want to have, um, well, you know," I replied with a shy squeaky voice.

"Whatever you're into, it's still a hundred bucks an hour."

"Perfect."

The redhead told us her name was Mandy, and said she was in.

Our other contestant was 6'2" in heels. She was African American with a blonde wig. Her name was Destiny, and she seemed the most intrigued by the idea.

"Let me get this straight, white boy—you gonna pay us $100 to race yo buddy? Just run down the street. And the winner gets an extra $100?" Destiny asked with a smile. "No sex?"

"Yes, ma'am," I answered.

"I'm gonna smoke yo cracker-ass," she said to Doug in a cackle.

"Bring it, sista," he said to Destiny while they performed a fancy handshake. Having married a black woman, Doug has considerably more street cred than the rest of us and can pull off high fives, chest bumps, intricate handshakes, and other activities that white guys normally struggle with.

We now had three contestants, and I had two chances to beat Doug.

Odds makers would automatically put the odds in Destiny's favor. She was black, after all, and as I explained a while back, white people are just not that fast. However, they had to race in their work attire, and Destiny had worn the six-inch heels that day, where Mandy had worn the more comfortable and conservative four-inch stilettos. We gave them time to stretch; they were stoked for time away from work, and the clock had already started, so they took their time and were hoping for time-and-a-half if the race went late.

A lot of bets were laid. Against my better judgment, I bet on Mandy, the white horse. I had a hunch. She had nice high calves, and appeared at least 80 percent sober. I was feeling confident with any bet against Doug. Along with the whiskey, I knew he had polished off an entire tray of pot-infused Rice Krispy treats. Plus, if you're not willing to lose a few hundred bucks watching your newly married friend race a lady of the night in his tuxedo, you're just a shitty, boring human being.

The race would be 100 yards of cobblestoned street. Our friend RiffRaff #2 paced off the distance in a stumble.

"Bring it," Destiny chided, already talking some solid shit. "Let's do this."

Mandy was silent; she had her game face on.

Doug took another shot of whisky for power (not that that makes any sense).

"On your mark. Set. Go!"

The ladies took off with impressive speed out of the gates and Doug had a small weed delay. I then noticed Doug still had lit cigar in his hand. After the wigs were adjusted, the second phase of the sprint commenced with Destiny showing that the six-inch heels and cobblestone street would not deny her the prize, although Mandy was hot on her heels with Doug neck in neck with her. When they approached the 75-yard mark, Destiny was getting winded and Mandy crept up. In a photo finish, Mandy took the Gold Medal in the Drunken Olympics. To date, there is still some argument as to who took home the silver medal. I actually think Doug came in second, but this will be the first time I've admitted that.

"I hate you, white girl," Destiny said with a smile. "I gotta get off my back and back in shape, girl."

Everyone involved was now hysterically laughing at the ridiculousness of the entire event. I did win the bet, but I gave my winnings to Mandy, and the rest of the crowd followed suit and rightfully gave all the money to Destiny and Mandy. Having made their quota for the week in less than thirty seconds, the ladies joined us for a few drinks and an early morning trip to the Waffle House. We went buck wild on that Waffle House menu.

"Can I see your full menu?" Destiny asked the server.

"Sure thing, ma'am."

"There's a different menu?" I asked.

"Stick with me, white boy, you got a lot to learn."

I picked up the tab for half the wedding party, including the bride and groom, as well as two slightly sweaty ladies of the night. There must have been a hundred plates on our two tables, and somehow the bill did not crack a hundred bucks. How the hell is Waffle House staying in business? Maybe instead of sending Bono, we should send Waffle House to cure world hunger. They seem to have a real handle on things. Plus, Bono is coming at them as a snooty multimillionaire, whereas Waffle House employees are making minimum wage and treat everyone with the utmost respect, no matter of race, income, or how drunk or high they are.

I doubt this wedding will be featured in *Bridal* magazine (or *Sports Illustrated* for that matter), but at the end of the day, a wedding is just a party, and this one will be hard to top.

14

JESUS GOES TO BED AT 11:30

When I started my first book tour for *Where the Hell Were Your Parents?* I really had no idea what to expect. I figured it would be a somewhat civilized, classy affair, and it was for the most part, but given the fact that I, along with a lot of my readers, still insist *jank* is actually a word, I should have known there might be a few speed bumps along the way.

The party started in Bremen, Georgia, and the first book signing was at the golf course and so didn't include any fistfights or Jello shots. I hadn't spent any real time at home in two decades, and it was great to see a lot of familiar faces. There were a few takeaways from not seeing my hometown in twenty years.

First, cute ages better than beautiful. The cute girls I remembered from high school had aged well, very well, but the beautiful, popular girls were sometimes unrecognizable as

I embarrassingly reintroduced myself to childhood friends. This might be a genetic anomaly, or more than likely they were taken down a peg by Smokes, KFC, and Jack Daniels (aka the three horsemen). These three will knock the sheen off even the most luscious of fruit.

But it's not like the years have dodged me either. At forty, things just aren't as tight as they used to be. I've become a little self-conscious about the fact that if I turn too fast to look for oncoming traffic, my chin fat will make the same turn a split second later. There are a few options for Snuffleupagus neck. Plastic surgery, because as we all know, fake pretty is better than real ugly. But that's stupid. I'm not a male model or an actor, so it's not like my neck jiggle is cutting into my income. Or, I could just be a man and accept the ageing process with grace, and maybe grow a beard to duck blind the whole affair. The problem with growing a beard is that chins tend to breed and multiply under the foliage, only to come back like Obi Wan Kenobi, more powerful than you could ever imagine. And please, if you're one of these new hipster lumbersexuals, either buy an axe and learn how to use it or lose the beard. You're either a computer programmer or a lumberjack; these professions are mutually exclusive, you cannot be both.

Or the other solution I discovered for chitlin-neck on my tour was that, if I'm really concerned about my double chin, I could just hang out with dudes with triple chins. So I reached out to some of my old football buddies from Polk High to discuss our heroic four-touchdown game. These boys had been storing up Ls and Bs for over two decades, preparing for a potential famine in the case of a Super Walmart closure. If you're having any body image issues, I also highly recommend a trip to the McDonald's inside the Super Walmart. You'll walk out of there feeling like Brad Pitt in *Fight Club*.

My wife flew in and joined me for part of the book tour. I love traveling around The South with my wife; she's autistic when it comes to the subtleties of Southern communication.

"What kind of meat is the BBQ?" my wife asked the waitress, her first interaction on Southern soil.

"You ain't from here, are ya, honey?" the waitress answered, with her hand on my wife's shoulder in a sign of pity.

Before I married a Canadian, I truly did not realize the complicated nuances and half-truths we Southerners use in our everyday communication.

"I'm glad everyone liked the soup," my wife said, as our dinner party guests were leaving.

"What makes you say that?"

"What do you mean? Everyone said it was great."

"They have to say thanks and that it tasted great; that's just the price to play down here. You have to say something on top of that if you actually want to pay someone a compliment."

"So, nobody actually liked the soup?"

"We like to think of it as manners."

"That makes no sense."

"To you."

"*Nobody* liked the soup?"

My wife also brings her fanciest clothes in an attempt to keep up with the finely dressed Southern ladies. Southern women are famous for dolling themselves up, and let's be honest here, they look damn good. They're fun to look at, but you'd never marry one, they're all as crazy as a badger in a washing machine for the most part. My wife will also dust off her makeup bag in an attempt to match her Southern counterparts' facial reconstructions. I truly believe I could be riding a pogo stick and still apply makeup better than my wife. She looks like a raccoon dressing up for Halloween. Luckily, I like it that way. I've never quite understood why women paint a fake face on top of their real face. Eventually, I'm going to see you without makeup, so why don't we fast-forward to that day, and save us a lot of time. What if I showed up to a date with a George Clooney mask on? You'd be a little disappointed when I finally had to slide it off, right? My wife also stands out in The South because she has short, naturally-coloured salt and pepper hair. This haircut always leads to confusing questions about sports.

"You play softball?"

"Uh, no. Why does everyone keep asking me that?" she answers, confused.

"Run track?"

"No. I'm a forty-year-old woman; there's not really a track team for middle age women that I'm aware of."

My wife explaining her career to Southerners is one of the small pleasures in my life. It's a conversation bomb, similar to my Little Johnny's Birthday joke. When she tells people she's a midwife, they slowly walk away from her, careful not to turn their backs on a real-life fucking witch. It gets me every time.

My wife really does have the social graciousness of a young

Jackie O (and yet is ironically married to me). However, there is one thing that does trip her up down South: The Good Book. She'd have a hard time telling you the order of the Testaments, much less pulling specific scriptures.

"Just like it says in Luke 3:14," a man said to my wife at a pool party.

"I'm not familiar with that passage, can you remind me what it says?" my wife will answer, in a gallant effort to continue the conversation smoothly. But every time, she inevitably paints herself into a corner.

"Just look it up on your phone."

"Excuse me?"

"Your phone, just look it up on your phone."

"The Bible is on my phone?" Along with not being a Biblical scholar, my wife is not the most tech savvy person (which I say as a compliment, by the way).

"You don't have the Bible on your phone?"

"I'm not sure."

This is where she starts glancing at me to come and save her with a fishing or hunting story. I always want to save her from her plethora of Southern social faux pas, but the urge to be entertained by her is far greater. I'll get a slap on the shoulder when she's finished, but it's worth it.

After my wife left the book tour, there was one awkward moment at a signing when a table of high-society ladies began questioning my morals (as they relate to Jesus obviously). First, there was some debate about the word 'hell' in the title of my book. Hell is mentioned around fifty-four times in the Bible, and I just assumed it was the official cuss word of the Bible. But I was told firmly that this was not the case, as one woman placed her hand over the title in order to not see my blasphemy. I just cringed, thinking about the plethora of four letter words on the inside of the book that were going to singe her finely manicured and alert eyebrows.

Now of course, this belle wasn't actually offended. She just wanted everyone to think she was, in order to keep her place in the social pecking order at her bridge game. First she scolded me for not wearing my wedding ring, as if this ring of metal is a force field that prevents me from entering women other than my wife. It's jewelry, not electric shock therapy. Then she started in on the evils of cussing.

She bought two books, so I played along with the ruse. I brought up the fact that there is nothing in The Good Book that says I shouldn't cuss; it might make me look kind of stupid and a bit of a hack writer, but it wasn't spiritual. She quickly pointed out the God's-name-in-vain commandment, which I was smart enough to avoid in the first book. I decided not to mention that I had recently discovered that my sons, having never stepped foot in church, *only* know the Lord's name in vain.

"Jesus!" my youngest yelled after stumping his toe.

"Do you know who Jesus is?" I asked.

"Jesus is a person?"

And that is why my boys are not allowed on any book tours where steeples outnumber pubs. They think Jesus is just what their dad yells if he steps on a Lego (aka rookie dad land mines). I'm a little concerned about them burning in hell for eternity while I bask in top water stick baits and chocolate malt milkshakes in heaven. On many occasions I've considered taking them to church, as I would miss them in the hereafter, but every Sunday I end up selfishly trading my kids' eternal souls in for an afternoon of fly-fishing.

"I'm pretty sure most cuss words were invented after the Bible was invented," I replied carefully, not wanting to cut into my sales.

"No, the Bible says a Christian should never use foul language," Ms. Bible School said.

"It does? Where is that—New Testament?"

"It's in there," Ms. Bible School answered, a little flustered after I put her on the spot to quote scripture. "I know it is. You cannot make jokes about Christianity."

"Really? I just figured if God was all knowing, that it also included humor."

"Not in this case," she answered sternly.

"Never? We never get to make a Jesus or God joke?"

"Never. Never. Never," was all she could say.

So if you can never joke about any aspect of Christianity, just throw Jesus in there with yoga, childbirth, vegans, Randy the Macho Man Savage, hard-core feminists, and anything organic as things that innately lack a sense of humor.

My twin brother Brian and my friend Ray even got in on the moral high-ground action while we were relaxing at the bar after the book signing.

"You really shouldn't have made that Jesus joke in the book," Brian and Ray informed me.

I know I've been away for a while, but now I have Brian and Ray, two of the most immoral heathens I've ever met, busting my balls because I made a few jokes. I took a look around to see who was in earshot.

"You know your wives can't hear you right now," I whispered as they both glanced around the room to double check. I leaned in. "Listen you two little shits, I knew you way before your wives did—your second wives, I might add—and I know the things you two like to pretend you didn't do, not the cute Huck Finn shit that's in the book either. I know the stuff you don't even talk about with each other when you're alone. Pistol whipping, jacking cars, underground casinos in churches, B & E, gambling trips to Biloxi ..."

Ray quickly cut me off. "I actually loved the book, and would highly recommend it. How about you, Brian?"

"It's amazing, the next *Gone with the Wind*," Brian answered in a sarcastically serious voice, as he toasted our beers.

And then came a text from what would become the after party. And I quote:

Bitch ... When you get done with high society, why don't you bring yo pussy ass up here and see if you can drink with us girls!!!!!

Once I figured out who sent the text, and where she was, I knew I might need to pack some penicillin, a spare liver, and a solid alibi. The text came from a high school friend, and she was drinking up at the Double Nickel.

The Double Nickel is for drinkers what a cardboard box is for homeless people. It gets the job done fast, easy, and affordably. The building also doesn't appear to be much sturdier than a cardboard box. Having not seen the place in over two decades, I figured it would have changed somewhat. I was wrong. The ceiling was still missing the same tile in the corner, where twenty-five years ago a good ole boy lit it on fire in protest when someone attempted to play George Michael on the jukebox. The place was like looking into a time capsule: same people, same decor, and the same thick blanket of smoke, this despite the fact there is now a law against smoking in bars in Georgia. But if you need to know one thing about the ole Double Nickel, it's this: the Double Nickel does not give a shit. Period.

As I walked in, the odds of me getting my ass kicked had instantly risen, but for some reason, I was finally relaxed. The classy charade Southerners put on for each other had faded away, and the only thing left was the bourbon-soaked marrow, similar to Thoreau's marrow, but not nearly as self-righteous, self-involved, or boring.

Just after midnight, as luck would have it, I was now sitting on a couch with one of the high-society women from the book signing—Ms. Bible School herself. She was still giving me the gears about my lack of wedding ring and how that was a sign of infidelity. My wife also doesn't wear a wedding ring or an engagement ring, mainly because she could lose a crippled hippopotamus in a bathtub, and also because I spontaneously proposed to her and thankfully never got around to buying her a small expensive trinket.

But now, four hours later, and in a different locale, and with a different drink (the white zinfandel had been traded for tequila on the rocks in a plastic cup), Ms. Bible School's moral high-ground was quickly eroding. As I mentioned, even with a BMI in the at-risk range, I'm still considered anorexic for a middle age man in this neck of the woods, and the ladies were starting to notice. I've also been past the county line a few times, so I'm a bit of a novelty when I come home.

Of course, to outsiders I still insist that "God talks like we do" when people question my accent, so I ain't exactly Benedict Cumberbatch. (Lewis Grizzard wrote the first funny book I ever read. Many uneducated heathens around the world have not heard of this great man. And in his honour, I drop this dime on anyone who questions my accent. I think as a humorist. There are very few timeless jokes, and this Lewis Grizzard gem is a keeper that I want to keep in circulation.)

"So Mr. Author, I think it's time you and I head back to my place," Ms. Bible School yelled over "Tennessee River," which I'm pretty sure has been playing on loop since 1994. Calling me an author is like calling Willie Nelson a casual weed smoker. But I do like the idea of being an artist; my idiosyncratic personality then might be seen as peculiar and unique. As a non-artist for the past forty years, I've just been a twitchy, emotionally unstable, stressed out, inappropriate weirdo.

"Uh, weren't you saying I was an immoral heathen a few hours ago?"

"Don't be such a prude, everybody knows Jesus goes to bed at 11:30."

I was somewhat taken aback by the specificity of the cutoff time for kosher extra-marital affairs. I'm not a regular churchgoer, so this tidbit could have easily slid by me.

"I'm assuming that's New Testament?" I asked. "But still, I'm pretty sure my wife would be pissed."

"Why do you have to be married?" she said in what I've discovered is the official slogan of a woman letting you know that she will indeed sleep with a married man.

Ms. Bible School then, deep in thought, took a strong drag on her Marlboro Red, which she had pulled out of her purse (despite the fact she insisted she did not smoke).

"Well," she purred, "she'll not care if we just make out on the couch."

I've since dissected this statement many ways. Did she mean, "Just *make out* on the couch," as in if there's no penetration my wife would surely not mind? Or, did she mean, "Just make out on the *couch*," as in what happens on the couch, stays on the couch—kind of like Vegas? I really had to go out on a limb and say that my wife would be upset at both second and third base, as well as fondling on the couch, or any piece of furniture for that matter.

When I first got married, I even had a hard time cheating on my wife in my dreams, which is completely moronic. There is nowhere in my vows that says I can't dream about playing naked twister with women other than my wife while I sleep. I think my wife must have drugged me. As far as I'm concerned, when I'm asleep, our marriage is open, very open. But now eleven years into marriage, my conscience has relaxed.

"You were giggling in your sleep. What were you dreaming about?" my wife asked.

"Uhhhhh, fishing?"

"It was sex, wasn't it?" For the record, all my dreams fall into three categories: fishing, sex, and zombies. I guess my sleeping brain can only handle three subjects.

"Yes."

"Was I in the dream?"

"Of course, honey, just you and me under the covers, just the way I like it," I'll say as we both roll over knowing that I'm lying through my teeth. But what am I supposed to say? Should I tell her that I had just picked up a hitchhiking Natalya, who recently defected from her Mother Russia Gymnastics team and is willing to do *anything* for her freedom? That would just be rude.

The night progressed, and the crowd was getting to where they wanted to go and the Karaoke machine was fired up. I found it somewhat ironic that a bar that was originally built as an Amvets post to welcome home the vets of World War II would now be serving up Japanese style sing-alongs. I hate Karaoke, and avoid it like gonorrhea.

"You're up next there, hot shot!" the bar owner yelled at me. This was not a lady I wanted to argue with, so I figured my best option was to negotiate a bit and we compromised on me doing a little stand-up routine.

I got up and was doing my bit about Organic Tampons, and considering how drunk everyone in the place was, it felt like I was killing. I even had a heckler, which was cool and I was letting him have it.

But then he yelled at the bar owner to "Shut the fuck up!"

I'd been drinking quite a bit at this point, and I stopped

my bit about Vegan Vaginas. I remember slowly thinking in my mind, "Huh, I remember when I lived here, if you talked to a woman that way, you'd get your ass …"

Bam! Before my Jack-Daniels-soaked IQ could process the thought, the good ole boys were beating the poor hell out of the man right at the foot of the stage. This is where you realize who the real men are. Real men step forward. I had now subconsciously backpedaled to the bathroom, with microphone still in hand, not even sure how I got there. A group of heavyset men then heaved the poor man out into the gravel like a sack of corn, only to calmly return to their seats.

"Tell us another joke, thar, funny boy," said the scariest man in the group, as if he'd just returned from the bathroom.

"Yes, sir!" I said quickly, trying to remember if I was to the Kermit the Frog part of the bit.

As the sun began to rise over the giant oil tankers drifting across from the Double Nickel, I found myself contemplating Jesus. If the Son of God went to bed at 11:30, what time did He wake up? Jesus strikes me as an early riser—people to feed, water to walk on, miracles to perform, eggs to hide—so I'm guessing he's up by 6:00 am at the latest. That gives us 6.5 hours of guilt-free transgressions every night. Like a year around Ramadan, if you hired Caligula as your activities director. And because we are all 'officially' Methodist and Baptist, we do not have a hip confessional booth to drop off our sins like a bag of hammers. I guess each time the sun comes up we automatically get a fresh scorecard. So all we have to do is keep our shit together for 17.5 hours, and then we can get our freak back on. I think I can handle that.

15

SODOMY, WHAT IS IT GOOD FOR?

It looks like gays will now be able to marry in all fifty states. And thank goodness, because it was starting to make me nervous. I'm not gay, that's not the issue, and I'm not about to start spouting off my own political beliefs, as I like to sell books to all of 'Merica, not just the half that agree with my point of view.

However, the idea that someone could lose a civil right if they violated the word of God left me feeling a little uneasy. Besides gay marriage, the Bible has a lot to say about other aspects of marriage (and life), and if biblical scholars start breaking down the Old Testament phonetically, some of us might end up deported to North Korea to mine corn.

Pre-marital sex is an obvious one (*1 Corinthians 7:2*). With 95 percent of Americans violating the word of Paul, this is by far and away our most favorite scripture to write off as a typo.

It is worth noting that religious beliefs only account for 1 percent of the virgins, the other 4 percent are the people who understood *Lord of the Rings* before the movies. But imagine if 95 percent of Americans, after having pre-marital sex, suddenly lost a civil right, like the right to hold public office. So obviously I'm concerned, not only for myself, but for this great country. Imagine a country run by virgins. That sounds about as exciting as a fishing trip with Richard Simmons.

Divorce is mentioned over a dozen times in the Bible, but it's still a coin-flip if you'll take part in this sin (*Matthew 5:31-32, Mark 10:2-12, Luke 16:18, etc.*). Bam, there goes another 50 percent of the population that might lose a civil right, like the right to drink alcohol. So you accidentally married a bat shit crazy woman the first time. It happens, but you at least need a nice handle of Makers to wash it down with. And what's divorce without its partner in crime, adultery, which could take out another 20 percent of the population *(Exodus 20:14)*. Adulterers might be forced to use separate bathrooms (it's really the only sanitary solution for these heathens).

We do not want to go down this rabbit hole, folks. When we break out the abacus at the end of the day, there's just not that many of us left.

And women have it worse, as they must fulfill their marital duties (*Corinthians 7:1-16*). Personally, I like the sound of this one, but I don't know if my wife would agree. So, let me get this right, if my wife doesn't have ass on tap, she might lose a civil right, like the right to bear arms? She should at least be able to use a black powder musket and a bowie knife to defend our house—I mean, we're not Canada.

On top of this, her body belongs to me and her breast must satisfy me always (*1 Corinthians 7:1-16 and Proverbs 5:18-19*). Can't question the Bible—sweet Jesus, the possibilities. I've always had a thing for redheads, and lately I've been into tattoos. I don't mean to question the Bible, I'm just saying that if we are going to really start enforcing the rules, I'm going to have to clean up my act and maybe ease up on my bottomless bucket of shrimp habit *(Leviticus 11:12)*.

Which brings us to the most uncomfortable, and least probed, verse of the Bible—Sodomy (*Gen. 13:13*). This one gets confusing fast, and on many levels. Sodomy, aka Butt Sex, sounds harsh to my tender ears and for the sake of this story, I will be referring to it as the "forbidden love."

At first, it seems straightforward—another solid reason to maybe throw some gay dudes in jail. But then the water gets muddy. I did a bit of a straw survey and close to half of my straight guy friends are also into the so-called forbidden love. Now these aren't all bankers and lawyers, but these aren't face-tatted, perpetually unemployed men either. This is something to keep in mind when we start enforcing The Good Word. Gay men only make up 2 percent of the male population, but if we start kicking this hornets' nest, we might lose another 49 percent of all men (and obviously 49 percent of women as well). I do find it interesting that whenever a politician is discussing withholding rights for gay people, they tend to use two men as their example; they are strangely more comfortable with the idea of two women sleeping together.

And then, we have the idiots.

There is a new troubling trend among today's Christian youth. Normally, I don't rag on the next generation's music, baggie pants, or stupid haircuts. Who am I to judge? I grew up in the '80s with parachute pants and a veg-head. But the combination of sexual fear mongering, lack of sex education, and just downright lying to our kids about sex has led to a *very* odd trend.

This one is going to hurt a wee bit, and I'm really not sure how to make it more comfortable, so let's just thrust straight ahead.

There is a popular trend with today's Christian youth to *only* participate in the forbidden love, because this way they're able to remain "virgins."

<Cue confused look on the face of anyone born before 1990>

Feel free to take a brief commercial break if you need a breather.

Who the hell says? Who are these idiots trying to fool? Jesus? Their first husband? The gynecologist? This makes absolutely no freaking sense on any level.

If you think this is normal behavior, let me break this down for you—you are an idiot. A complete fucking idiot. You are as dumb as a sack of chickens. It's better you heard it from me than the man upstairs.

Peter: "Welcome to heaven. Sorry, but I can't let you in, you've had pre-marital sex?"

Idiot: "No I didn't, I only had anal sex. That doesn't count."

Peter: "Uhhhh. Who says?"

Idiot: "I read it on the Internet."

Peter: "What's the Internet?"

Idiot: "Well, that's what Billy said."

Peter: "Is Billy an apostle?"

Idiot: "Well, no."

Peter: "You're also going to hell for being gullible and stupid. Incidentally, you'll be penetrated against your will for eternity downstairs."

So you hit a homerun, sprint around the bases, but then when you get to home plate, you cleverly two-step over it straight into a porno? If you hit a grand slam, it's still a homerun. And you think you're still a virgin? Really?

I just don't get it. If you were driving to New York, the city of lights, the city that never sleeps, the city where you can have a wooden crate of Czechoslovakian beer, a bag of Bugles, and a dime bag of weed delivered to your door at any time of day (rumor has it), why would you detour and beeline it straight for Cleveland? Cleveland is okay I guess, but compared to New York, it's a bit dirty and rusty, don't you think? There are just so many things you can do in New York, the food, the activities, the shows; I can hang out there for weeks. Cleveland is the Dairy Queen of fine dining, you might think you're having a good time, but afterward, you just feel dirty, violated, and have a mysterious lower abdominal pain.

And, I'm not saying you should never visit Cleveland. Lebron went back, but keep in mind there was a few millions dollars on the table. And if you say you wouldn't "go to Cleveland" for a million bucks that means you're either lying or you're too stupid to know how much a million dollars is.

Kids: just have normal sex. Trust me. Contrary to what they tell you, your parents had pre-marital sex, and most likely with people other than the folks you call Mom and Dad. Just because your dad looks like an effeminate Ron Jeremy today doesn't mean he couldn't lay it down back in the day. Hell, for that reason alone you should be bumping uglies: time is ticking. You've already lost your virginity, even if you're too stupid to know it: you're just doing it backward. So do us all a favor, flip over, and go have some normal, safe sex. You can send me a thank you letter later.

And, who amongst us has never coveted thy neighbor's house with the indoor/outdoor pool, or admired a friend's man slave. Hell, even my lovely wife has admired our neighbor's miniature donkey. She loves that little ass.

16

THE INCONVENIENT TRUTH ABOUT MEN

Like most of us, I've helplessly watched several friends' marriages implode. A couple of years ago, I decided I'd sat on the sidelines long enough, and I set out to solve this major issue. If not me, then who? Sure, there are smarter and more qualified people to solve this problem, but through countless years of research at poker tables, fishing holes, bars, garages, hunting camps, and mud bogs, I have actually discovered the one surprising fact that will guarantee you a happy and successful marriage. More about that later.

I have also made two secondary discoveries about successful marriages. The first is that a spouse should never write a book or appear on television and say they know the secret to a perfect marriage (smartass short stories appear to be harmless). Anyone who has the audacity to stand up and proclaim their marriage to be the ideal to strive for is a delusional egomaniac. Just think of John Edwards, Elliot Spitzer, Jessica Simpson, and of course, poor Kathy Lee Gifford who told the world about her perfect union daily until her husband was caught doing the plough in a hotel room that featured a vibrating bed (RIP).

My second accidental finding is that unless it's your twenty-fifth or fiftieth anniversary, a husband who publicly proclaims his love for his wife over loud speakers is banging one or more of the secretaries at work. It's assumed you love your wife: you might seem to remember some vows you declared back when you had hair and a 32 inch waistline. Think about it this way: what if your wife, while flipping pancakes onto your plate, adds, "I didn't poison your coffee today." Wouldn't you be a little suspicious? But these discoveries are trivial compared to my real breakthrough.

Recently, I returned home to find five cars parked in the driveway. For safety, I decided to tiptoe through the back door. As I entered I was overwhelmed by eight high-pitched, obviously chardonnay-soaked voices stacked on top of each other. It sounded like a cockfight; and the cocks were losing. From the safety of the laundry room, it didn't take me long to figure out that one of the participants, a lady named Susan, had walked in on her husband screwing a Hooters waitress.

"Hooters? Are you serious? I can't fucking believe it," one voice squeaked.

"With those dumbass shorts and veiny boobs?" yelped another on top of her.

"I know. I know. It's just so unbelievable," Susan went on.

"Girl, you gotta ditch his stupid ass," the dogpile continued.

"There's no excuse for that shit."

"I'm just in shock," replied Susan, with an overly dramatic sigh as if someone had just murdered her family with a machete. "I truly can't believe it."

Next to a woman's wedding, getting divorced is the second highest source of attention she'll see in her lifetime, and Susan was soaking it up. Only two of the eight women were still with their first husbands—one of whom, surprisingly, was my wife.

Every morning I am ecstatic and surprised to see that my wife hasn't left me. Before she really even has a chance to wake up, I'm quick to cook her a nice breakfast with a cup of tea. The way I see it, if I try to get by on my personality, wealth, and charm, I am destined to come up short. I just feel it would be damn hard for a woman to walk away from a hot cup of tea and an omelet.

But anyway, if you're on your second husband, or especially your third, shouldn't you bow out of a conversation on marital advice and maybe focus on making the margaritas?

Normally, this would be the end of the story. Man cheats, wife catches him, and her friends paint their faces and start delivering speeches like William Wallace trying to get alimony. However, there is more to this story, as there usually is, which is where my research began.

I happen to be close friends with the philandering husband. For the record, it is true; Dave R. (who I would just call John Doe if I weren't such a dick) was screwing Ms. Curly Fries. But what Susan the Victim skipped over during her diatribe of nonsense was that she had not had sex with her husband in over a year when the event occurred: twelve months, eight days, seven hours, and twenty to twenty-three minutes depending on how you work the stopwatch. Is it *inconvenient* that Dave had sex with Ms. Curly Fries? Absolutely. Is it *unbelievable,* as the drunken flock proclaimed? Of course not.

As we all know, stuff like this happens: we men tend to stick our dicks in things. It's an affliction. A man's first choice is the person who is geographically located the closest to him; it's purely sprinkles on top if he also happens to like that person. If his first choice is taken away from him, he'll turn to option two: porn. Porn innovation makes Steve Jobs and Apple look like a monkey with a hand full of feces. I mean, you can have a live video chat with an actual woman in Bangladesh, who happens to be into Crisco and knee-high socks. It's gone so far now that 2D Playboys can be sold in Christian bookstores.

Susan had not only locked up her cookie jar; she had also installed a porn blocker on my buddy's computer like he was a fourteen-year-old boy. He was forced to go old school and buy *Jugs* down at the local truck stop. How humiliating.

So Dave was not allowed to play with his starter, and the bench was technologically off limits. Meaning, his wife had forced him into free agency. Who's in free agency? Well, everyone basically. Your neighbor, your sister, your mom, your best friend, the neighbor's farm animals, furniture, and Ms. Curly Fries sure as hell makes the list.

On top of this, he had to routinely do the nod-and-sigh at group functions when his wife and friends would discuss being in their sexual prime as middle-aged women. With the advent of the PC police and a new wave of feminism, it is now socially unacceptable for a man to ever disagree with a woman in a public setting. Mix this with men's attempt to never cock-block a buddy, and women can now pretty much say any nonsense they want and get away with it.

When it comes to women's sexual prime, I'm going to say what we all know: middle-aged women are not in their sexual prime. All men know it, and women know it as well, even if you don't admit it. And I'm not saying middle-aged men are in their prime either; men age like milk, and by the time we hit forty, we start to look like a gorilla who's been kept in captivity too long. Women are in their sexual prime at twenty-four, give or take a few hours. And if you're now doing the angry face and grumbling, "I am in my sexual prime, you asshole," I'll defend my position in three easy bullet points:

1. You're telling us that you just so happen to hit your sexual prime on the exact day you could no longer cry your way out of a speeding ticket.

2. We have this thing now—it's called the Internet. You can actually look up bullshit facts to see if they are true or not.

3. In the history of planet Earth, there have been roughly 54 billion men on Earth. To date, nobody has yet located one, not even one, oversexed middle-aged man.

"What's wrong, Bob? You look exhausted."

"It's Susan. She's wearing me out. I had to go down on her for an hour last night. She wants threesomes, costumes, and all the positions! I just can't keep up."

Yes, it sounds ridiculous, because it's never been said. So

ladies, please quit insulting our intelligence with this nonsense. Middle-aged women are beautiful, whatever, but to make us beg for booty while simultaneously telling the world that you're in your sexual prime leaves us stuck in a hamster wheel of suck.

And we all know that the rules of engagement change as you get older. A forty-year-old man or woman is not coming to the plate for a single, double, or triple. You're either waving me around the bases or please do not call me up to the show in the first place. Just leave me in the dugout where I can spit seeds in peace. I haven't hit a double since I unsuccessfully tried to lead a Jehovah's Witness astray back in the early '90s. She's now forty, married, and, I'm assuming, finally having sex. I bet she, along with other religious virgins, kick themselves once they're married and figure out exactly what they were giving up—I have the same relationship with weed.

But don't sweat it. With my one-step plan you will avoid this shit-show and live in a state of marital bliss not seen since *The Waltons*.

How to be a perfect husband? Not a damn clue. Maybe clean up your shit, don't get fat, ditch the video games, and don't tell stupid golf jokes.

How to be a perfect wife? This is much easier. Women are overthinking the issue, and you're giving men too much credit: you need think Cro-Magnon. Women are bombarded by useless information by 'experts' in self-help books, daytime talk shows, and magazines, all of which are trying to sell their crap. The real solution is worthless, which is why Oprah bought it back when she was rocking shoulder pads and an afro and has hid it under her bed in a lock box ever since. But I am here to set you free.

So here it is. Ladies, you better get out your notepads, diaries, Blackberries, iPads, iPhones, smartphones, crayons, Etch-A-Sketch, whatever you need to write down the bomb I am about to drop on you.

Fuck the shit out of your man three and a half times a week.

There it is. You got it. My job is done here. No more *Cosmo* surveys, no more marital advice books written by women, no more hour-long talk shows with thirty-five minutes of commercials.

Now, I don't mean married our-socks-and-t-shirts-are-still-on sex, I mean the real goods. Remember when you used to take the *other* person's clothes off? You'll need to bring the junk you did back in college; you need to make his toes cramp. This is the fornication you had back before sexy time with your husband was replaced with Facebook scrolling. It might seem horribly unfair that the onus of a perfect marriage falls 100 percent on the wives' shoulders, but that is how the research panned out. And I'm not saying it's a wife's duty to have sex with her husband. But it works out in the end, as the spinoff benefit more than makes up for it. Get your pencils back out, write this down:

if you are taking it to your man three and a half times per week (in the way we both know you can) you can do whatever the hell you want to do for the rest of your life.

ANYTHING! Want to go to New York with the girls? Done. Want your husband to asphalt the driveway in July?

Done. Girls' night out on every weekday that ends in Y? Done. He will not have the energy or desire to leave the couch except to make sure you are content in every way. Dishes done, clothes washed, meals cooked, kids taken care of, diapers changed, new car, vacations, it's all at your fingertips. Quit bitching and go get what's yours, girl. There is research that shows the opposite is also true, that a man doing chores is a turn-on for women. But let's quit this Who's On First nonsense, it's time to get down to business.

If you are wondering how to have sex 0.5 of a time, it's either the average of three one week and four the next, or well … you know.

As part of this limited time bargain, I am offering a 100 percent money back guarantee on my free advice. Ladies, if you take it to your husband for a month and your marriage does not drastically improve, I will refund all your money, no questions asked.

Husbands: if the plan doesn't work, and you get to ride the mechanical bull for a month without having to put quarters in it, feel free to send fly-fishing gear, a handle of Knob Creek, or at least buy my book, and we'll call it even.

17

MIC DROP

As a single man, I fancied myself as a bit of a Johnny Appleseed of penis—I was not a good person. Men don't ever say this, but it's painful to look back at our single selves. We were just so damn stupid, the shit we thought women liked. It's ridiculous. And about the time we figure it out, we're off the market, which explains the dearth of male talent on eHarmony. If a twenty-year-old man only knew what a forty-year-old man knows, well, he'd be dead. But, he'd be a fucking legend.

Looking back, the cooler I thought I was at the time, the more of an ass I was in reality. And now, I truly know I am not cool, and I'm not fishing for a compliment or hinting that I'm actually cool now. It's impossible to be cool with this much ear hair. So at some point, theoretically, I would have had to cross over the parabola and actually have been cool.

I've thought about this quite a bit lately; when was I actually cool? I've ruled out everything pre-1998 and after 2005, so I've narrowed it down to an eight-year gap in my life. I also know I was never cool for a full year, or even a month, so most likely I'm looking for a single day where my clothes, haircut, and personality were all socially acceptable.

One of the days that I thought might have been the day was back in 1999. I was cooking dinner for some nice looking ladies, when I took a break from the fish tacos (which I had caught) to save a deer that was caught in a fence, without burning the tacos. I would say that was the pinnacle of my coolness, but later that night, I got drunk and almost sliced my thumb off trying to open a beer bottle with a sword. So that day's out.

Or once, at the request of a five-year-old boy, I killed a quail at twenty-five yards with just a rock. That was pretty cool, until I realized I was camping with some hardcore vegans, who were not nearly as impressed as the five-year-old (who mercilessly plucked the little McNugget right in front of them).

Now, after a decade of pondering this riddle, I think I know the day when I was, in fact, cool.

Throughout my life, I've never thought very highly of myself, but dressed up with a stern face and a clever joke I can look the part of a confident asshole. Or at least I used to when I cared enough to put that much effort into the act. Back in the day, I tended to soak my self-esteem in carnal pleasures, which can occasionally lead to disaster—but let's be honest, nothing peps up a shitty Wednesday night like a nice open-mouth kiss from a complete stranger.

One day, on the lead up to a potentially hedonistic weekend, I had dared my mutt-like stomach to ingest milk from a rusted can. When the proprietor of the tea-stand went to pour it in my cup I was fearful of botulism, but my Southern manners prevailed and I accepted the drink with a smile and a thank you. And for some dumbass reason, I actually drank the potion. After a few minutes my stomach began to hurt, but I was still able to go about my normal day-to-day activities with only a few extra trips to the bathroom.

The next day I had planned to run a half marathon. I was not only running, but I was also one of the organizers, and thus felt obligated to take part in this random show of endurance we white people tend to do for no apparent reason. My stomach was almost back to normal when the race started. It wasn't easy, but my sphincter prevailed and I ran the entire race without incident. My big-boned body limped into the finish line in a full clinch, and straight to the bathroom. After a little bit of rehydration, I started on the celebratory beers. After I had polished off a dozen or so, my body started convulsing, letting me know that I was done. I was extremely drunk, beyond exhausted, and still fighting off rusted-can syndrome. A little after midnight I hobbled back to my house and then, just as I got ready to lay my damaged body to bed, a truck drove up.

In the truck was a very cute woman, who was not nearly as drunk as I was. I had been spending a little time with her lately and I had a bit of a crush on her. We worked together, and had even kissed once or twice while working the night shift at a high school. Our job had been to stay up and make sure the kids were not snorting Ritalin. ADHD is a killer, and the sickle cell of the white upper class.

We struck up a casual conversation on the front porch and then she asked if I'd like to come home with her. Not only was this woman cute and interesting, she was also a landscaper. Now I'm not a fetish type of guy, but if I were, my fetish would be landscapers.

I know this sounds strange to my Southern readers who are now picturing me gazing longingly at Mexican men in Car-harts. That's not what I'm talking about. In other parts of the world, specifically the Pacific Northwest, other races and sexes can cut grass. Even white girls! Girls slave away in the smoldering sun wearing brown leather work boots, bright colored socks, short blue jean shorts, white tank tops, and bright orange safety vests. They're sweaty, dirty, and have rough hands and muscular bodies. They shake hands like a man, and when they hug you it's hard to breathe and you just feel safe and somewhat threatened at the same time. There's no nail polish, and you can tell they just cleaned the dirt out from under their nails. There's just the right amount of soft white fuzz on their upper thigh. Wait … where were we?

A gorgeous, wonderful woman had asked me to go home with her. But I was in no condition to go, so I made the obvious decision.

"Sure, I'd love to," my ego said for me.

Fuck! That is not what I meant to say. My body was beyond done. What was I thinking?

The night progressed fine—in those days I could easily

operate heavy machinery with a dozen beers in me with or without rusty can syndrome—and finally, the sleep rolled over me like a slow wave of heavy lava. I have never slept so deeply in my life. My legs were still twitching from the run as I fell asleep, drunk and happy.

And then at 2:43 in the morning my life changed forever. I woke confused and startled, and had no idea where I was. I looked around and all I could see was the bright red digital 2:43 in the corner. It took me a second, but I figured out I was in her bed, but I was still confused as to why I had awoken so suddenly. I've always had nightmares, so waking up breathing heavy and sweaty is not out of the norm for me. But this was different.

My forehead was drenched in cold sweat. I looked over at my new friend who was snoring quietly. She snored in that way only cute women can, where it's charming and kind of sexy. Men just can't do that. I then felt a wetness in my crotch area. It was too wet and too thick to just be sweaty balls. After shaking the cobwebs from my brain, I quickly figured out what had happened.

Mud butt.

Now, I'm not some drunken frat boy. This had never happened to me before, and has never happened since. But the one time it did happen to me, I happened to be lying with a beautiful woman and not even wearing boxers for damage control. To say I panicked is an understatement. I quickly grabbed what blankets and sheets I could, and retreated to the bathroom. I left the woman lying alone, shivering, on the base sheet. I had not only soiled the bed, but also this beautiful woman. This was not one of my finest moments.

Now 100 percent sober, I was going through all my options. There was a shovel in the truck, nobody had seen us leave together and we were in the middle of nowhere. I could just bury her in the swamp and nobody would ever know.

No you can't, you fool! Your DNA is more than everywhere, and you can't kill a perfectly good white girl and expect to get away with it.

Think, Nathan, think, you fucking idiot.

I was pacing the bathroom like a caged tiger. I then threw all the covers and sheets and myself into a scorching hot shower and removed the lid from the shampoo and dumped it all over the blankets. The bubbles continued to grow as I left the shower running on top of the sheets as I dried myself off and returned to the scene of the crime.

As I came out of the bathroom, my new friend had shivered awake. She was now putting two and two together, and although horrified, was doing a helluva job allowing me to save face. However, there was no amount of omertà that was going to swear this woman to secrecy and I was not ready for the world to find out I was a grown-ass man who shit the bed.

And then, in a great moment of clarity and vision, I had what will go down in my obituary as the greatest idea of my life. I knew what I had to do.

I walked up to the soiled bed, in just a towel, cooler than Arthur Fucking Fonzarelli and got down on one knee. This wonderful creature, who was just barely awake, rightfully stared at me in confusion.

"Will you marry me?"

We'll be celebrating our twelfth anniversary this year. What's the traditional gift for being married twelve years? Sheets?

ACKNOWLEDGEMENTS

First and foremost, a huge thanks to my wife for allowing me to endlessly test material on her. You rarely laugh, but you also never slap me, and I can live with that. I'd also like to thank Jody Carrow, my editor, who reviews my manuscript without judgement, and never makes me feel stupid for my loose understanding of the English language. Evan Pine, you once again have provided a stunning cover design. And thanks to the Promontory Press team for pulling it all together.

And lastly, thanks to anyone who has ever laughed at one of my jokes, it means more to me than I can explain.

ABOUT THE AUTHOR

Nathan Weathington is the author of *Where the Hell Were Your Parents?* and *Invasion of the Bastard Cannibals.* He has a bachelor of Civil Engineering from Auburn University and an MBA from the University of Victoria.

He has worked as a civil engineer, bartender, math teacher, secretary, GM of UsedEverywhere.com, founder of PostaNote.co.nz, and the publisher of several newspapers in British Columbia. As an up-and-coming media mogul, he responsibly decided to ditch his career to pursue the untold riches of becoming an author.

Nathan grew up in Bremen, Georgia, a small rural town that serves as the backdrop for his first book. While living in The Bahamas, he met his Canadian wife. He now lives with his family in New Zealand, where he pursues his obsession with fly fishing.

www.ingramcontent.com/pod-product-compliance
Lightning Source LLC
Chambersburg PA
CBHW061759070526
44586CB00023B/2635